THE BRIDGE

How to Launch Your Career through a Legal Internship

THE BRIDGE

How to Launch Your Career through a Legal Internship

Maxwell D. Rosenthal, Esq.

LexisNexis

Print ISBN: 978-1-6328-1810-2

Library of Congress Cataloging-in-Publication Data

Rosenthal, Maxwell D., author.
The bridge: how to launch your career through a legal internship / Maxwell D. Rosenthall, Esq.
pages cm
Includes index.
ISBN 978-1-63281-810-2 (softbound)
1. Law--Study and teaching (internship)--United States. 2. Law--Vocational guidance--United States. I. Title
KF282.7.R67. 2015
340.071'55--dc23 2015032572

Editorial Offices
630 Central Ave., New Providence, NJ 07974 (908) 464-6800
201 Mission St., San Francisco, CA 94105-1831 (415) 908-3200
www.lexisnexis.com

MATTHEW BENDER

(2015–Pub.3400)

Dedication

To our son, Nathan.
May you find purpose and happiness and your life's work.

Acknowledgments

A wise man once told me: "Success is achieved by working hard and surrounding yourself with people who are smarter than you." I truly have taken this advice to heart. While writing this book was essentially a solitary endeavor, I was supported in myriad ways by a community of intelligent, experienced, dynamic, generous, enthusiastic, and insightful individuals. For their help, I am eternally grateful.

First and foremost, I must thank my beautiful and brilliant wife, Rosanna. You are the centerpiece of my world — a wonderful mother to our son, Nathan, my best friend, toughest critic, and biggest advocate. You make me a better father, husband and professional and fill my life with passion, purpose, and laughter. I deeply appreciate all of the sacrifices you made so I could write this book.

Next I would like to thank my family. I was blessed to be raised by loving parents who encouraged me and my siblings to support and appreciate one another, and to be unafraid to try new things. Without this warm upbringing, I would not have had the confidence to attempt to write my first book. I owe a special thanks to my older brothers, Joshua and Michael, who, on one lazy Sunday afternoon three years ago, enthusiastically engaged in the brainstorming session that inspired this book.

Very early on in this journey, Ari Kaplan and Julie Schechter gave me advice that helped me transform my raw ideas into a book and avoid many obstacles along the way. Thank you for your time, encouragement, and charity. Without you both I'm not sure how far this would have gone.

At different junctures while writing this book, I sought input from a "panel" of legal professionals working at law firms, in-house legal departments, government agencies, and law schools who all selflessly reviewed and gave feedback on the content of *The Bridge*. For their contributions, I would like to recognize, in no particular order: Adam Turbowitz, Esq., Justin Steinfelder, Esq., Benjamin Wilson, Esq., Greg Skiff, Esq., Heather England, Esq., Matthew Monteith, Esq., Nathaniel Christian III, Esq., Maura Kelly, David Rossi, Esq., Coleen Chin, Esq., Marc Antonecchia, Esq., Anne Gibbs, Linda Morton, Esq., John Erbes, Esq., Andrew Krinsky, Esq., Jeremy Paul, Esq. and Luke Bierman, Esq. Your insights ensured that *The Bridge* would benefit all law students and, on a personal note, reaffirmed my confidence in the collective good nature of our legal community. Thank you for taking time out of your packed schedules to add value to this endeavor.

Many thanks to the team at Lexis Nexis, Keith Moore, Kimberly Brennan, and Teri Smith, for their excitement for *The Bridge* and collaboration throughout the process.

Last, I'd like to thank all of my colleagues at Tarter Krinsky & Drogin LLP, especially Alan Tarter, Esq. Andrew Krinsky, Esq. and Laurent Drogin, Esq. (the "wise man" quoted above) for teaching me by example how to be an honorable attorney and professional, providing me with the platform to run TKD's legal internship program, imparting your wisdom and guidance on me, and consistently supporting my career.

Table of Contents

Foreword

By Cliff Ennico

There have been many changes in the U.S. legal profession in the 35 years since I graduated law school. I am happy to have instigated some of them.

But one thing — a BIG thing — has not changed. Talk to any legal recruiter, or law school placement person, and they will all tell you the same thing: "it has never been harder to land a legal job, especially for recent law school graduates."

It is no secret that law school, like medical school, doesn't teach you any practical skills. As it was 35 years ago, you spend most of your time reading cases and (maybe) do some moot court stuff. If you're lucky, you have participated in some sort of legal clinic. If you're even luckier, you have written for your law school's Law Review or other more specialized legal journal. But if someone asks you to draft a will, form a corporation or limited liability company, or help them buy a new house . . . you're clueless.

Like young doctors, young lawyers traditionally have served an "apprenticeship" period following law school. They would work as an "associate" (read, employee) for a law firm, "learning the ropes" and immerse themselves 100% in legal work under the tutelage of more senior lawyers in the firm until they can stand on their own feet and handle cases, business transactions, and other legal work without supervision. Our profession has never called it "internship and residency," but they might just as well do so. It was never easy to land these "associate" positions, even 35 years ago, but today it is nearly impossible.

But here's one thing that has changed in the last 35 years: back then there were no "internship" positions as such. By "internship" I mean something akin to a "work study" program in other professions, where you can get your degree and work X hours a week at a (mostly unpaid) job in the hopes that a job offer will be extended to you upon graduation.

The biggest development in legal career management since the 1980s is the proliferation of "internship" positions — both paid and unpaid — at law firms, corporations, and other legal employers. The minute you start attending law school, you have to begin thinking about how you will get a job upon graduation. Waiting until the summer after second year may well be too late – the good positions may well have been taken. Landing the right "internship" during your law school years, and possibly immediately afterwards, may well make the difference between a successful legal career and working as a barista at Starbuck's.

In the 35 years since I graduated law school, there has not been a single book published in the United States to help young lawyers find and deal with internships. Now there is one. In this book Max teaches you the "real world" of legal internships, and gives you the "inside baseball" you will need to survive and enter the "holy of holies" of our profession — the right full-time position upon graduation.

You should thank your lucky stars that my good friend Max Rosenthal has written this book. He didn't have to, after all. He could have kept all he learned to himself, left you to figure out how this world works, and joined the legions of lawyers (you will meet many) who feel that mentoring the next generation isn't important.

Instead, he took the time and effort out of his 90-hour-plus workweeks to write a wonderful book about how to get, and survive, a legal internship. Because he cares about you. He really does. And amazingly, despite all hard evidence to the contrary, he remains stubbornly optimistic about the future of the U.S. legal profession, and your future in it.

He reminds me of another young lawyer I knew once.

CLIFF ENNICO

(www.legalcareer.com),
author of "The Legal Job Interview: Winning the Law-Related Job in Today's Market", "Business Lawyer's Handbook: What Business Lawyers Do", "Partner Track: How to Go from Associate to Partner in Any Law Firm", and the forthcoming "Bathrobe Lawyer: How to Build a World-Class Solo Law Practice from Your Home Office."

Introduction

Whether or not you realize it, beginning on the first day of law school, chances are that you committed yourself to becoming an attorney. You have only three years to figure out what kind of attorney you want to be and best position yourself to become it. Use this time wisely.

Take comfort in knowing that you made a great decision to attend law school. Upon graduation, you will join a community of professionals working at the center and highest ranks of business and government. You can choose to work for many types of organizations, including law firms, in-house legal departments, government agencies, the legislature, public advocacy groups and the judiciary. You will have the honor and responsibility to advocate on behalf of others, counsel on matters of importance, seek justice, reach resolution and impact change. Indeed, practicing law can be prestigious, exciting, dynamic, fulfilling, lucrative and fun.

But many challenges also lay ahead for you. For one, regardless of whether you have signed checks or promissory notes, law school is an enormous financial commitment, the impact of which will not be felt until after graduation. And once you do graduate and are fortunate enough to land that first job, you will likely be working long hours. This means that the quality of your life after graduation will depend heavily on whether you enjoy your work. Make no mistake, the time to start building your career has already begun.

Don't waste another minute looking back and questioning your decision. Rid yourself of all hesitancy, tentativeness and doubt and fully commit to this endeavor. Start thinking strategically about what you must do to set yourself apart from your peers, further your professional maturation and enhance your marketability upon graduation. If you do this, there will be a profoundly rewarding career available to you – but nobody is going to hand it to you. You must reach out and seize it.

The Bridge is about empowerment. It's a blueprint for obtaining the legal internship that is best for you and using that experience to take control of your career. My hope is that reading this book will provide the clarity, confidence, motivation and direction to bring you closer to achieving success, whatever that means for you.

CONTENT DEVELOPMENT FOR *THE BRIDGE*

My internships during law school were profoundly positive and transformative experiences for me. I grew immensely through the challenges presented, learned a great deal about what I wanted (and did not want) in my legal career and developed relationships with attorneys who now are some of my most esteemed colleagues. I credit much of my professional successes to the strides taken and seeds planted during my legal internships.

While it didn't happen straight out of law school, I eventually returned to the organization where I spent my final internship. Along with practicing law, I also designed and now direct my firm's legal internship program. I spearhead the recruitment, interviewing, hiring, supervision, training, mentoring and evaluating of law students who work at our firm year round. I draft and post our job openings, review resumes and cover letters, coordinate and conduct interviews, make hiring decisions, work closely with our interns, give mid-way and final performance reviews, and participate in high-level discussions about whether to hire them as attorneys.

Through this process, I have learned the common intern mistakes, challenges, misperceptions, and observed and helped them overcome obstacles to achieve success. I've paid close attention to how interns interact with other attorneys and support staff, watched them struggle and improve, and stayed in touch with them after they graduate, search for attorney positions, enter the workforce, and become my professional colleagues.

Working with law students has become an integral part of my daily life and a source of great satisfaction in my career. My own internship experiences, along with my work as head of my firm's internship program, served as the motivation for authoring *The Bridge* and the foundation for its content.

The Bridge is rooted in extensive research and incorporates principles from various disciplines including human resources consulting, recruitment and relationship-building, professional development, leadership training, experiential learning, behavioral, cognitive and organizational psychology, and law practice management. These principles are applied to real situations that arise during internships to provide color, context, foreshadow what to expect and to resonate with the reader.

The lessons of *The Bridge* were then refined with the input of law school career development administrators, practice management professionals, and practicing attorneys with decades of work experience. To ensure that *The Bridge* addresses internships in all sectors of the legal industry, a panel of practitioners from small and large law firms, federal and state government agencies, non-profit organizations and in-house legal departments was enlisted to review, edit, and approve the material.

The Bridge covers every angle, is endorsed by legal professionals of all experience levels and sectors and, perhaps most importantly, addresses the issues that apply to legal interns today. It is relevant, comprehensive, and practical. The guidance set forth in *The Bridge* is designed to optimize any internship experience.

Reading Considerations

A couple points to keep in mind as you read. First, the word "internship" is a blanket term used throughout this book that refers to any practical legal experience, paid or unpaid. Irrespective of whether it is a formal program facilitated by a school or a part-time job found on Craigslist – the lessons in *The Bridge* apply to any arrangement where a law student is working in a real world setting. In that regard, "internship" encompasses whatever term is used by your school for these arrangements, such as externship, fellowship, clinic, practicum, cooperative, clerkship or summer associate.

Second, *The Bridge* is written primarily for the vast majority of law students who plan to practice law after graduation in some capacity. Careers outside the practice of law are too varied to be taken into account in this book and if you plan to be a non-practicing lawyer, there may be certain principles that don't apply. Overall, however, *The Bridge* will benefit any law student who is about to embark on an internship, regardless of their post-graduate aspirations.

Third, the instructions in *The Bridge* are not a precise recipe. You do not have to do *everything* exactly as directed in order to succeed. Rather, this is a comprehensive exploration and illustration into *what you should do* to achieve success in obtaining and performing during a legal internship. As you read, don't become overwhelmed if you feel like you can't do everything that is recommended. But know that the more you do, the greater your chances will be for success.

STRUCTURE OF *THE BRIDGE*

The Bridge has a natural order to it and, if appropriate, should be read in its entirety from the beginning. Part I opens with a two-tiered inquiry that should be conducted by every law student as early in their career as possible. Chapter 1 is an internal exploration of what a law student should be considering about themselves when determining their career path. Chapter 2 then turns the student's inquiry outward to a comprehensive overview of the various job options within the legal profession. Part I is a pre-requisite for making large decisions about your legal career, one of which is selecting where to work as an intern.

Part II walks through the three, equally-important stages of obtaining your legal internship – finding, applying and interviewing. Chapter 3 demonstrates how to strategically-focus your search to find the greatest number of attainable job opportunities, your ideal position and/or an internship that puts you in the best position to get hired for your ideal position in the future. Chapter 4 explains how to draft and seamlessly weave together a narrowly-tailored resume with an eloquent and endearing cover letter. Chapter 5 prepares you for delivering a great performance during your interview to seal the deal and get the job offer.

Part III sets the three goals for your legal internship. Chapter 6 travels the stages of the Experiential Learning Cycle and instructs on how you can acquire the most practical legal skills. Chapter 7 explains how and why you should strive to create working relationships with attorneys during your internship. Chapter 8 defines professional development and identifies the various experiences during your internship when it is most likely to happen.

Part IV is a game plan for successful performance. Chapter 9 shows you how to prepare to meet the specific challenges that you will face during the internship. Chapter 10 encourages you to always be enthusiastic and how intrinsic motivation can help you overcome adversity. Chapter 11 highlights the importance of demonstrating a strong attention to detail and provides tips to avoid making mistakes. Chapter 12 explores the difficult situations that may arise and provides techniques for managing your stress. Chapter 13 introduces the concept of upwardly managing your supervising attorneys and applies its principles to the internship/assigning attorney relationship. Chapter 14 provides a step-by-step process through which you should nail your research assignments. Chapter 15 lists twenty of the most impactful tips for successful performance during an internship. Chapter 16 walks through the final tasks of ending your internship right.

PART I:
DETERMINING YOUR CAREER PATH

Before searching and applying for your legal internship, pause a moment to appreciate the gravity of this decision. This is an important junction point in your legal career. Think it through before taking action.

Law school is filled with important decisions. You choose which elective courses to take, clubs and associations to join, journals to write for, events to attend, books to read and/or relationships to develop. These decisions, along with your academic performance, will ultimately define your law school experience and set the stage for your professional career. But the most important decision you will make in law school is not one of these, but rather, where you will work during law school — your internships.

Before making this decision, it is imperative that you map out your career path. You can do this by boosting your awareness in two interrelated areas: (1) who you are; and (2) your job options within the legal field. First, in order to fully grasp who you are, you should evaluate various career-oriented considerations such as your values, interests, desired lifestyle, financial needs and personality. Keeping in the back of your mind what you know about yourself, turn your inquiry outward to explore the sectors, organizations, practice areas and industries in which you can pursue a legal career. Consciously make note of what you uncover in the process and what areas merit further investigation.

Going through this two-tiered analysis will enable you to confidently and thoughtfully set realistic career goals that are aligned with who you are. Only after this is accomplished should you be searching and applying for a legal internship.

Chapter 1

YOUR CAREER CONSIDERATIONS

We are all unique and possess a distinct combination of values, interests, financial needs, desired lifestyle and personality. It is these attributes that should dictate what career path is best for us. Put another way, we must truly know ourselves before we can credibly set our own career goals.

And we should get to know ourselves as soon as possible. You will always have the freedom to modify your goals down the road. But the farther you travel down a particular career path, the more obstacles and resistance you will face if you try to change direction.

This principle remains true for all law students, regardless of their school or class rank. Even the most accomplished law students can find themselves struggling to find happiness in their professional career because they did not recognize what was best for them. No matter who you are, if you fail to appreciate and be guided by your uniqueness, you risk heading down the wrong path.

This chapter is designed to dispel any preconceived notions that you may harbor about your career goals by conducting an internal inquiry into your uniqueness. It should be the first step to selecting your career path and revisited each time you are making any career-oriented decision, especially where to work during and after law school.

Be Patient

Law students sometimes have tunnel vision when choosing their career. They seek to avoid the discomfort of indirection by impulsively selecting a path without first understanding themselves or surveying what else is out there. This can be a big mistake.

At some point, there is usually some experience that compels a student to pursue a particular direction. For instance, students frequently chart their initial course as a result of:

- Having successful work or academic experiences prior to law school;
- Becoming impassioned during an in-class debate;
- Excelling in a particular course;
- Meeting with a professional who speaks inspiringly about a particular career;
- Enjoying a volunteer experience at an organization or event;
- Knowing someone who can make getting an attorney job easier;

- Joining a club filled with like-minded classmates; or
- Becoming intrigued by a speech, panel or discussion.

Other students simply determine that they will be happiest making the most amount of money and working at a prestigious institution.

Be wary of relying solely on these considerations when selecting your career path. All of them are valid. But they are also one-dimensional and may overlook critical factors. Thus, they should not lead to conclusions, but rather provoke further questioning and exploration to confirm what is right for you.

Remember: You didn't go to law school to simply get a job. You went to get the best job for you. Stay true to that goal. Don't just jump into the first opportunity or path that seems promising. Hold out, be patient and take the time to thoroughly think through what path will lead you to a successful and enjoyable career.

> *Do you think you know what you want to do once you graduate? What experiences or beliefs led you to reach this decision?*

YOUR "STORY"

At the onset, it is important to recognize that, with each decision you make, you are writing the "story" that will become your career path. With many job applications in your future, you must be sensitive to what this story will sound like. Will your experiences tell a story of a focused, passionate professional who knows what he or she wants to do? Or will your story be about a student who kept changing their mind because they haven't figured out what they want to do? The latter story may make potential employers nervous about your commitment level and be an impediment to getting hired.

While you should be actively pursuing any and all avenues to increase your marketability upon graduation, you must also be carefully crafting your "story." You want all of your decisions during law school — elective courses, groups, journals, competitions and, of course, internships — to weave together seamlessly into a cohesive, linear career path. This is not always the case. But it is ideal. And the more honest reflection and exploration you make early on in your career, the less anomalistic experiences you will have to explain away on your resumé.

> *Can you sum yourself up in one sentence in a way that sets you apart? What story does your resumé tell? Are there experiences on your resumé that are outliers or negatively impact the image you want to portray to potential employers?*

YOUR VALUES

It may be difficult to truly understand your core values until they are violated. But everyone has values that should be understood and appreciated when selecting a career. Misalignment of values with a legal career can cause discomfort on a daily basis, conflict in the workplace and overall dissatisfaction. On the other hand, performing work that furthers your values can bring tranquility, pride and gratification to your career.

> *Have you ever been in a situation where you felt your values were violated or mismatched with what you were doing? How did it feel? What specific values were implicated? How did you handle it and move forward? Have you been taking into account those values in your career decisions so far?*

There are many values to be pursued in a legal career. These values can be broken into two categories: what you want to achieve and who you want to serve. Go through the following exercise to help uncover what is most important to you as a professional. Make note of your results.

1. **What do you want to achieve?** On a scale of 1 to 10, rate the importance of the following career accomplishments:

- Helping people in a direct way
- Contributing to the betterment of the world
- Working at a reputable organization
- Having power and authority
- Influencing the attitudes and opinions of people
- Competing with others
- Accumulating large amounts of wealth
- Gaining public recognition

Not every legal job presents the opportunity to achieve each of the above accomplishments. Instead, there are tradeoffs that must be made when you select a particular career. Distinguishing between the achievements you are willing to give up and those that are a "must have" in your career will help illuminate your best-suited career path.

> *Based on your responses above, what values are most important to you? Are you pursuing a career path that is aligned with these values? If not, what would be a step in the right direction?*

2. **Whom do you care about serving?** Think about who you want to represent as an attorney and answer the following questions. Make note of the answers.

Do you want to represent individuals in their personal affairs? For example, trust and estate work for families, representing children in juvenile proceedings, representing spouses in divorce matters, bringing personal injury lawsuits on behalf of individuals who have been harmed physically or emotionally, or defending individuals charged of crimes. ***Yes? What type of personal affairs? Why?***

Do you want to represent companies in their business affairs? For example, counseling executives on how to properly hire and fire employees, representing real estate developers in purchasing properties or bringing infringement lawsuits on behalf of patent holders. ***Yes? What types of businesses? What types of affairs? Why?***

Do you want to represent the interests of the public generally and work to impact social change? For example, you could work for non-profit organizations that lobby for changes in legislation or bring lawsuits to fight for civil liberties on behalf of groups of individuals. ***Yes? Which members of the public? What communities? What type of social change is most important to you? Why?***

Your values can be shaped by your moral, personal, financial or cultural affinities. They are an integral part of who you are and must not be disregarded or undervalued at this early stage in your career.

Your Preferred Lifestyle

Your quality of life after graduation will largely depend on whether your job permits you to live the way you want to live. Again, accepting that you cannot have everything and there must be tradeoffs, consider the following lifestyle considerations. Rank which ones are most important, and ask yourself the specific questions. Make note of your answers and, just as important, the questions you are unable to answer right now.

1. Financial Security — How and how much you want to be paid? Some organizations have less financial stability but offer the possibility to make large sums of money at once. Other companies, firms or government organizations pay steady salaries with predictable, lockstep raises. There's no correct answer; only the answer that best fits your personality and financial situation.

- *Do you want to be paid a steady salary?*
- *Do you want bonuses, increases in compensation based on client origination, merit raises, or stock ownership in your company?*
- *Do you want stable health benefits?*
- *Would you be stressed out if your cases were taken on contingency fee basis?*

2. Job Stability — At their core, companies are nothing more than a group of people working together to achieve a common objective. Some companies are tied together more firmly, while others are loose associations that can change or separate quickly. Some government agencies or non-profits expand/contract their workforce based on the political landscape or availability of government funds. Other companies have existed for centuries and rarely lay off employees.

- *How much risk do you want to take in your career?*
- *High risk and high reward type endeavors?*

- *Large organization with established structure and proven longevity?*
- *Small organization with more upside but less stability?*
- *An organization funded by grants or project-based?*

3. Work/Life Balance — Some people work to live; others live to work. Most are somewhere in the middle. Achieving balance between work and personal endeavors is a central ingredient for physical and emotional health, maintaining positive relationships and overall happiness.

- *What sort of control over your work hours do you want and how much do you want to work?*
- *Long or short hours?*
- *Fixed schedule or flexibility?*
- *Work from home or office?*
- *Unpredictable schedule?*
- *What do you want to do before work? After? Weekends?*

4. Work environment — Most lawyers spend a large portion of their life in the office. It is important that this time is spent in a work atmosphere that suits you, which depends on the people, office structure, types of clients and organizational culture. If there are certain types of work environments that are incompatible with your desired lifestyle, do not ignore this insight.

- *What sort of surroundings do you want to work in?*
- *Busy, fast-paced office or calm, quiet and predictable?*
- *Do you want to work in groups and collaborate or work alone?*
- *Do you want to have one boss or many people for whom you work?*
- *Do you want to work in a corporate, business-like culture or more relaxed, congenial work environment?*
- *Do you want to have co-workers who are competitive and primarily concerned with their work or more congenial, social and friendly co-workers?*

5. Location — Some people have ties to a particular region. Others have little or no connection to a geographic area and can be open to job opportunities anywhere. If you know where you will eventually be settling down, then you should try to find an internship in that area. If you are not tethered, then evaluate the pros and cons of different cities, states, countries and try to narrow down the best spot for you.

- *Where do you want to work?*
- *What kind of weather do you want to live and work in? All four seasons?*
- *Do you want to live in close proximity to your family or friends?*
- *Do you want to live in culturally-rich or diversified areas?*
- *Do you want to live near mountains, oceans or lakes?*

Your Interests

If you are in law school it is natural to assume that you are interested in logical analysis, intellectual challenge and the rule of law. But this, again, is merely a starting point. There are many other interests that you may be able to make a part of your career. Here a few examples:

- If you are interested in the political process, government regulation or public policy, consider pursuing a career in administrative law, civil rights or working at a government agency.
- If you are interested in visual arts, consider a career in-house at a production studio, practicing in intellectual property or entertainment law, or representing artists, photographers, filmmakers, painters or actors.
- If you are interested in architecture or the notoriety of landmark physical structures, consider a career representing designers, architects, general contractors or real estate developers in their construction and real estate legal matters.

Legal work touches on all aspects of life. While your role will always be to provide legal services, involving yourself with interesting people, topics and problems will increase your job satisfaction. And it is possible that, as you develop a deep understanding of certain industries, your legal counseling may eventually cross over into industry-specific business advice.

What interests you? Technology? Engineering? The elderly? Politics? Traveling? Life sciences? Event planning? Public relations? Would you like to make these interests part of your career and deal with them on a daily basis?

Your Financial Needs

The common thread of the majority of law students is that they have spent or borrowed an enormous amount of money to pay for their legal education. The ABA reported that, in 2012, the average debt for three years of law school is $122,158 for private school graduates and $84,600 for public school. If you have taken out loans, do you know what your monthly loan payment will be after graduation? This must be taken into account when forming your career goals.

As an illustration, consider the following table with the estimated minimum monthly payments for different loan amounts at different interest rates, based on a 20 year term:

Loan Amount	**Minimum Monthly Payment with 4% Interest Rate**	**Minimum Monthly Payment with 6% Interest Rate**	**Minimum Monthly Payment with 8% Interest Rate**
$50,000	$302.99	$358.22	$418.22
$100,000	$605.98	$716.43	$836.44

Loan Amount	Minimum Monthly Payment with 4% Interest Rate	Minimum Monthly Payment with 6% Interest Rate	Minimum Monthly Payment with 8% Interest Rate
$150,000	$908.97	$1,074.65	$1,254.66
$200,000	$1,211.96	$1,432.66	$1,672.68

These figures are only intended to present a rough estimate of your potential minimum monthly payment. And these payments will increase/decrease depending on the duration of the payment term, whether you opt for a loan forgiveness or income-based repayment plan (consult with your school's financial aid office) or whether you elect to pay more than the monthly minimum. Regardless, your student loans will be a fixed cost that follows you wherever you end up after graduation. You must embrace this reality.

Now consider that the average starting salary for all lawyers in the U.S. was $70,000 as of 2013, according to the job site Indeed.com. This average, however, can go up or down based on region or sector. The average is also misleadingly inflated by the small percentage of first-year associates at large law firms who actually earn six-figure salaries.

The following table breaks down an annual salary into monthly gross income and net income amount based on an estimated 33% income tax/deductions:

Annual Salary	Gross Monthly Income	Net Monthly Income
$40,000	$3,333	$2,200
$50,000	$4,167	$2,750
$60,000	$5,000	$3,300
$70,000	$5,833	$3,850
$80,000	$6,667	$4,400
$90,000	$7,500	$4,950
$100,000	$8,333	$5,500
$110,000	$9,167	$6,050
$120,000	$10,000	$6,600
$130,000	$10,833	$7,150
$140,000	$11,667	$7,700

Now subtract your estimated monthly minimum payment from your expected monthly net income. How much money is left over for food, rent, entertainment and other fixed/variable costs of living? Are you comfortable with this?

The decisions you make during law school can impact your financial situation after graduation. This is something to keep in mind while you are forming your career goals and charting your path.

> *How much student debt do you have? What is your estimated minimum monthly payment? Is it realistic to expect that you will be earning a six-figure salary after graduation? What is the most realistic estimate of your monthly net income? Are the decisions you are making during law school taking into account your financial situation after graduation?*

YOUR PERSONALITY

While most law students have already committed to a career in the legal field, there are still many decisions to make regarding the *type* of legal career to have. And the degree to which your personality matches your selected legal career is a big factor in whether you will actually enjoy your work. Thus, you should know your personality before selecting your career path.

While there are many ways to measure and assesses one's personality, consider taking a personality test such as:

- The Myers-Briggs Type Indicator (www.meyersbriggs.org);
- The DISC Assessment (www.discprofile.com); or
- The Kolbe Test (www.kolbe.com).

These personality tests are used widely to help individuals evaluate what career is best for them based on their natural tendencies, how they process new information, their strengths, weaknesses, preferences and other innate characteristics that impact their work performance and enjoyment in different environments. You can only benefit from gaining a deeper understanding of your unique personality, especially at this early stage in your career.

> *Have you ever taken a personality test before? What did you learn about yourself? Are you an extrovert or introvert? Are you a detail-oriented thinker or conceptual thinker? Are you comfortable brainstorming or prefer definitive answers? Do you base your decisions on past behavior or present, tangible concrete information? Or are you interested in future possibilities and underlying theories? What else do you know about your personality?*

YOUR CAREER GOALS

Now that you have evaluated the different aspects of what makes you and your situation unique, it's time to confront a series of overarching questions designed to help identify the general direction of your career path:

What are your overall career goals?

What is the path to achieving them?

What type of organization do you want to work at?

What type of role and position do you want to have?

What practice area do you want to concentrate on?

Write down the answers to these questions in pencil. But don't stop there. Before writing over with pen and marching forward on this path, inquire further into your navigational capabilities. Challenge your credibility with additional questions:

How have you arrived at the answers to these questions?

What research have you done?

Do your career goals align with your values?

Will your chosen career path provide you with your desired lifestyle?

Will your financial situation be sufficient if you pursue your chosen career path?

Are you truly interested in this position? Industry?

Do your personality traits dictate that you will enjoy and thrive in this role?

Your answers to the questions above — or difficulty in answering them — should give you an indication of the internal and external exploration that must still be done before locking in your career path. But, at the least, if you honestly and thoughtfully went through this internal analysis, you should now be ready to explore what is out there for you.

Chapter 2

YOUR OPTIONS IN THE LEGAL PROFESSION

Now it's time to turn your inquiry outward and explore the job options in the legal field. Combining self-awareness with a comprehensive understanding of the opportunities within the practice of law will allow you to select and proceed confidently down a well-suited career path. This, in turn, will enable you to find the right internship.

The following sections are an introduction to the practice of law. While there are exceptions to each generality set forth below, it is prudent to gain an initial familiarity with the unique characteristics of different legal careers.

These next sections should help to spark interest, clear up confusion or dispel misperceptions that you may harbor about what lies ahead for you. But it should not be the end of your research — only the beginning. Use this information as a launch point for further exploration.

The Practice of Law

In the most general sense, attorneys are problem-solvers. They examine legal issues in the context of the constantly changing law in order to find practical solutions for their clients. Attorneys can wear many hats, frequently shifting between counselor, mediator, negotiator and advocate. In all of these roles, however, attorneys possess the unique power to impact the rights of others, speak on behalf of their clients and act as agents of change. They work hard to acquire and retain this power and, as "officers of the court," are charged with the responsibility of ensuring that it is not abused by themselves or other attorneys.

Another hallmark of the legal profession is the special relationship attorneys share with their clients. Much like the doctor-patient relationship, the attorney-client relationship enjoys some of the strongest protections of any profession. These protections allow attorneys to learn confidential and sensitive personal, financial and business information, which they rely upon to handle matters of the highest importance to their clients, such as issues involving their money, business and personal liberties. Acting as a legal representative is a profound honor and serious responsibility.

This is where the commonalities within the legal profession end. Beyond this, there is a virtually endless variety of organizations, sectors, locations, practice areas, sub-specialties and industries in which attorneys may spend their career. The clearer your understanding of the characteristics, operations, pressures, problems, people, work environment and financial rewards associated with all the places where attorneys work, the better qualified you will be to find your own place.

ORGANIZATIONS THAT EMPLOY ATTORNEYS

Almost all practicing lawyers work at one of the following three types of organizations:

(1) private law firms,

(2) in-house legal departments, or

(3) public interest organizations (non-profits and government agencies).

This section will provide a brief overview of each organization type. As mentioned above, use this information as a starting point for further investigation.

> Side Note: In addition to becoming a licensed practicing attorney, law graduates also may pursue careers in a non-legal capacity at countless types of organizations. The most popular non-lawyer careers available to law graduates are an entirely different topic not covered by this book.

1. Private Law Firms

Around 70% of all practicing attorneys in the United States work at a private law firm. Law firms range in size from solo practitioners to firms comprised of thousands of attorneys with offices throughout the country and internationally. Some law firms specialize in only one practice area and others contain multiple practice groups. The many variations of law firms are endless. Below is a breakdown of the some commonalities and differences.

Commonalities Among Law Firms

No matter the size, practice area(s) or location, all law firms are united by one defining characteristic — they are private businesses that generate revenue by providing legal services to clients. Here are a three other hallmarks of law firms:

1. Billable hours — The "billable hour" is a law firm's method of measuring the amount of legal services provided to its clients. Simultaneously while they work, attorneys record the time taken to perform each task — typically in 6-minute increments delineated as 0.1 of an hour. Tracking time and being beholden to billable hour requirements can create a pressurized, efficiency-centric work atmosphere.

2. Client generation — Law firms operate within the service industry. This means that attorneys at law firms typically must engage in salesmanship, networking and relationship development in order to attract and retain clientele. If you view these activities as unpleasant and have no interest in them, you may run into certain barriers if you work in private practice.

3. Higher salaries — As explained below, salary ranges depend largely on the size and location of the firm. That being said, attorneys in private practice can *generally* expect to earn higher salaries than attorneys with their same experience level

practicing in-house or in public interest.

> Side Note: It is becoming increasingly commonplace for law firms of all sizes to use "alternative fee arrangements" ("AFA") with their clients in addition to billing on an hourly basis. Such AFAs might include flat fee arrangements, fee caps, project or portfolio-based pricing or some blend of the above. While this trend does not appear to have detracted from firms continuing to measure attorney production based on billable hours, it is nevertheless something for newer attorneys to monitor as they enter the workforce.

Large Law Firms (100 or More Attorneys)

Attorneys employed at large law firms tend to be the highest paid and most recognizable attorneys in their field. "Big law," as large firms are termed, typically have long-standing relationships with the largest businesses in the world and, consequentially, are able to charge the highest hourly rates. Moreover, large firms have the staffing capabilities to assemble teams of attorneys to handle the types of matters that major corporations frequently encounter, such as high capital, complex corporate transactions and extremely document-intensive litigations and investigations. Put simply, large law firms are built to service large companies.

Associates at large firms typically have annual billable hour "targets" between 1,800 and 2,300 per year. The following table demonstrates how these annual targets breakdown on a weekly and daily basis (factoring in 4 weeks of vacation):

Hours Per Year	Hours Per Week	Hours Per Weekday
1,900	39.5	7.9
2,000	41.5	8.3
2,100	43.75	8.75
2,200	46	9.2
2,300	48	9.6

Keep in mind these are *billable hours*, not working hours. It is commonly-accepted that it takes about 1.3 hours of "working time" to bill one hour. Thus, 39.5 billable hours requires working for 51.35 hours in a week and 48 billable hours equals 62.4 working hours. After factoring in time for sleep, eating, exercise and personal relationships, you begin to appreciate how all-consuming employment at a big law firm can be.

The obvious attractions to big firms are the training and compensation. There is a pedigree attributed to an associate with a few years of experience at a big firm. This perception makes them highly marketable. Furthermore, depending on the geographic location, first-year associate salaries at large law firms can range from $100,000 to $160,000 per year, plus there is sometimes the potential to earn an annual production-based bonus. There is, however, rarely an immediate financial incentive for associates to generate clients at big firms.

In sum, large law firms embrace a work-first lifestyle that does not cater to free time, maintaining personal relationships or flexibility in schedule. That being said, you can earn exceptional money at a big firm and leverage your marketability to smoothly transition to another position better suited to your desired lifestyle. No matter what your career goals may be, if you are willing to make the sacrifice, spending a few years at a big firm can open many doors.

Mid-Sized (10–100 attorneys) and Small Law Firms (1–9 attorneys)

Over 70% of all attorneys in private practice are employed at mid-sized or small law firms and, as the legal profession continues to adapt to economic changes caused by the Great Recession, that percentage continues to grow. In other words, if want a career in private practice, chances are that you will end up at a small or mid-sized law firm.

This category of law firms has varying billable hour requirements and compensation, depending on geographic location, management and practice area. For example, a three-attorney firm that practices Oil & Gas Law in Houston, Texas may pay their associates higher than a three-attorney insurance defense firm located outside of Portland, Maine. Or a personal injury law firm that takes cases on contingency-fee only will pay their associates quite differently than a boutique intellectual property firm. Therefore, assessing the lifestyle benefits and compensation structure of these types of firms must be done on a case-by-case basis.

Nevertheless, some generalities do exist. For one, smaller firms tend to have less overhead, such as fewer employees, smaller office space and lower marketing costs and infrastructure. This enables the firms to charge lower rates and set lower billable hour requirements for their attorneys. This equates to flexible schedules and better work/life balance for associates at smaller firms.

Compensation is typically structured as salary with potential merit-based bonuses. In addition, some small/mid-sized firms will reward associates who originate clients for the firm by paying them a percentage of fees collected from their originated clients or factoring it into an annual bonus. This possibility may make smaller firms more attractive to associates with strong interpersonal, marketing, networking and relationship-building skills.

Structure of Law Firms

Attorneys practicing at a private law firm hold the title of partner, counsel or associate. Each title delineates a distinct role at the firm.

1. Partner — Partners are at the top level of a law firm and their role is to develop and maintain client relationships or be highly knowledgeable in their practice area. Partners are extremely valuable to a law firm in that they originate business and act as the point-person in the firm being hired to perform legal services. Without partners, law firms would have no work and generate no revenue. Because of their experience and expertise, partners also make conceptual, strategic decisions on how to staff a matter, solve problems and achieve favorable results for the client. Partners'

compensation varies greatly from firm to firm, but is usually based, in some way, on the revenue they generate for their firm.

2. Associates — Associates are attorneys typically in their first to ninth year of practice. Their primary role is to service the needs of the partners. In a way, an associate's clientele consists of the partners at the firm and they are expected to perform whatever work necessary to service the partners' clients. Such work is usually detail-oriented, "nuts and bolts" tasks, such as research, drafting, preparation, and reviewing/analyzing documents.

3. Counsel — Counsel at a law firm (sometimes called "of counsel") is typically some hybrid of a partner and associate. Counsel typically have practiced more than nine years but do not have sufficient client relationships to become a partner. Depending on the size and structure of a law firm, counsel may eventually receive the partner title regardless of their clientele. Like partners, counsel compensation varies greatly, but is usually connected in some way to their production at the firm.

2. In-House Legal Departments

Larger companies will have in-house legal departments comprised of two or more attorneys, typically titled "general counsel" (partner-level attorney) and "associate general counsel" (associate/counsel level attorneys). Smaller organizations may have only a single in-house attorney. Unlike attorneys at law firms, in-house attorneys do not need to engage in the activities designed to attract or retain any other clients. They have only one client — the company.

> Side Note: There are also many companies that have in-house "compliance" roles. These roles don't typically require a law degree, but this is a whole new area for law school graduates to pursue, and it is a growing market. These roles are not necessarily practicing law, but can be a fast-track to an in-house legal position. The role of "compliance" differs from company to company, but the main responsibilities include corporate policies, processes, risk assessments, training, and monitoring company and employee behavior.

Regardless of the size of the company, in-house counsel will invariably need to be knowledgeable in the practice area that directly relates to the company's industry. For example, in-house counsel at a real estate developer will need to have some working knowledge of real property, title and land use law. In addition, most companies, regardless of their industry, inevitably encounter legal issues relating to their employees and commercial transactions. For that reason, in-house attorneys ordinarily have, at the least, a working knowledge of employment and corporate law.

The demands, responsibilities, goals and pressures of an in-house counsel position vary greatly by industry, company size and organizational culture. Some in-house counsel positions are one-dimensional, isolated roles relied upon only when business people seek approval before moving forward with a project or plan. Other in-house attorneys interact with all people throughout the organization and are involved in strategy and planning of business initiatives. Generally speaking, the smaller the company, the more dynamic the in-house counsel role.

Most in-house counsel typically work "regular hours" and have more control over their schedule than attorneys at law firms. In-house is often an attractive alternative career for attorneys who start their career at large private law firms and want to transition to a less-demanding work environment.

Law students, however, should be aware of a recent trend emerging for in-house positions. Companies seeking to cut costs have begun demanding more from in-house counsel and restricting the amount of legal fees they can incur from outside firms. In-house counsel positions at these companies will be just as, if not more, demanding than law firm positions.

In-house compensation is typically structured as salary/bonus and is generally lower than law firms. However, in-house attorneys can sometimes experience substantial financial gain by acquiring stock prior to a merger, sale or IPO. So there can be an enormous financial upside to an in-house job if you get in early at a growing company.

3. Public Interest Organizations

This is a very broad category and could be broken down into many sub-categories, but in the interest of this being a starting point for exploration, it is sufficient to describe public interest organizations as entities that aim to serve the public. These organizations operate in the private, government, quasi-government and non-profit sectors.

After private law firms and companies, the government is the next largest employer of practicing attorneys. There are varying levels of government where one can practice law, but the following is a general breakdown and a few examples:

- City/County: City Law Department, City Buildings Department, City Commission on Human Rights, City Solicitor Office, Department of Buildings, District Attorney's Office and Public Defender's Office.
- State: Governor's Office, Attorney General's Office, State Division of Human Rights, Counsel to House or Senate Committee, State Executive Agencies and the State Court System.
- Federal: White House Legal Staff, Military Legal Corps, Department of Justice, Federal Agencies, Offices of United States Attorneys, Armed Forces, Federal Legislative Aides, and the Federal Court System.

Attorneys practicing at these different government offices can do both transactional and litigation work. The practice areas are as varied as in private practice but can be quite specialized depending on the scope and jurisdiction of a particular agency or office.

Attorneys practicing for non-profit organizations may be engaged in advocacy on behalf of individual clients, a group of clients or may advocate for or against changes in the law. There is often an overlap in client-based and law reform work in the non-profit sector. In addition to these types of advocacy organizations, attorneys may also practice at labor organizations or philanthropic foundations.

Judicial clerkships and court staff attorneys are also a popular public interest careers. These positions present the opportunity to work alongside judges, act as mediators between litigants, and impact the law through the judge's decision-making.

Many people pursue a career in public interest to achieve the personal satisfaction inherent with working "for the public good." In that sense, many attorneys in public interest successfully align their values and career. But this comes with a sacrifice, as public interest jobs typically pay less than the private sector. Government benefits, on the other hand, tend to be top-notch.

Budgetary considerations limit the amount of training available and force public interest jobs to demand higher levels of responsibility earlier than that experienced by associates in the private sector. In other words, out of necessity, public interest offices embrace experiential learning for their attorneys. Such first-hand experience increases the marketability of junior public interest attorneys.

Public interest attorneys have no billable hour requirement or expectation to develop business. This makes public interest work more fitting for individuals who value work/life balance, flexibility in schedule and vacation time and who do not want to be spending their free time networking, building professional contacts or marketing their skills.

Practice Areas

Practice area is the single-most defining characteristic in one's legal career. It is the answer to the overarching question: "What *kind* of attorney are you?" And, for good reason — your chosen practice area will largely dictate your day-to-day activities, the types of problems you encounter, job stability, types of clients, work environment and lifestyle. Importantly, once you begin developing experience in a particular practice area, it is difficult to transition to a different one.

While further research must be done, the following are brief descriptions of some of the more popular practice areas:

1. Real Estate: Transactional real estate attorneys help entities and individuals acquire, lease and sell property. They do this by counseling and drafting commercial and residential leases, purchase/sale agreements, easements and other documents that deal with property rights. Some sub-practice areas in real estate would be landlord/tenant law, financing of construction projects or land use issues for real estate developers.

a. Real estate attorneys enjoy: publicity associated with large real estate deals; interesting public policy issues; the accomplishment of executing on a deal quickly and efficiently; appreciating the history and tradition of well-known property and buildings; close client contact; being able to see the tangible results of the legal work.

b. Challenges real estate attorneys face: tight deadlines; repetitive or routine transactions associated with compliance work; dealing with bureaucratic government agencies; unpleasant feeling of evicting someone from their home.

c. Real estate attorneys work at: law firms of all sizes; in-house at real estate developers, financial institutions, title companies, large corporations; federal agencies such as Department of Housing and Urban Development, Zoning and Planning Departments; non-profits dedicated to housing advocacy or community development; landlord/tenant courts, federal courts dealing with "takings."

2. Bankruptcy: This practice involves representing and counseling clients who are considering, going through or involved with bankruptcy in some way. Bankruptcy attorneys can focus on representing creditors and debtors, or act as trustees for the courts. Bankruptcy negotiations often take place when court intervention is likely and, therefore, knowledge of federal civil procedure, the Bankruptcy Code, and strong transactional skills are a must.

a. Bankruptcy attorneys enjoy: designing creative solutions to disputes over the disposal of assets; strategic thinking and negotiation; keeping companies in business and preserving jobs; valuation of assets; relying on business acumen to render legal advice.

b. Challenges that bankruptcy attorneys face: costly-adversarial litigation process; unpredictable judges; meritless arguments; overly-complex rules or unpredictable litigation schedules.

c. Bankruptcy attorneys work at: law firms of all sizes; in-house at banks, mutual funds, title companies, utilities and other companies that deal with finance; federal agencies such as Department of Justice: U.S. Trustee Program and the FDIC; state tax authorities; consumer rights organizations that have bankruptcy and debtor relief programs; federal bankruptcy court judges and staff attorneys.

3. Trust & Estates: This is a statutory-based practice area that aims to preserve wealth as rights/assets are passed down to generations and/or transferred within families. It entails drafting various estate-related documents such as wills, codicils and trusts, as well as working with probate courts and beneficiaries (sometimes with conflicting interests) to distribute assets according to wishes of decedents.

a. Trust & estates attorneys enjoy: not many deadlines; non-adversarial.

b. Challenges that trust & estates attorneys face: wealthy individuals are difficult clients to attract; the work can be boring; difficult to make partner; sometimes disturbing disputes amongst families.

c. Trust & estate attorneys work at: typically smaller, boutique law firms, probate court staff attorneys and judges.

4. Corporate: Corporate lawyers focus on the legal issues that businesses face. As this general description denotes, corporate law is an extremely expansive practice area that breaks down into many robust sub-practice areas, including mergers and acquisitions, asset finance, capital markets, general corporate, securities, private equity/leveraged buy-outs and structured finance. Common tasks include reviewing, drafting, filing with the government, and negotiating terms of transactional documents including various types of internal and external memoranda, ownership agreements between individuals and entities such as partnership/ shareholder/operating agreements, purchase/sale/assignment agreements and finance-related contracts.

a. Corporate attorneys enjoy: high-profile deals; helping businesses grow, evolve, acquire and protect their assets; intellectual challenges that require strong business acumen.

b. Challenges that corporate attorneys face: negotiations can become adversarial; very detail-oriented deals; compliance can be repetitive, routine work; deadlines can be short; clients can be demanding people with dominant personalities.

c. Corporate attorneys work at: law firms of all sizes; in-house at companies of all sizes; federal agencies such as the SEC, Department of Commerce, Department of Transportation, FDIC, Federal Reserve Board; legislative committees and sub committees; Attorney General Offices and city law departments; federal, state, trial and appellate court judges and clerks.

5. Tax: This area of the law is an extremely complex, regulation and rule-centric practice and typically requires an LLM. Tax attorneys navigate federal and state/local tax issues and can counsel individuals on estate-related issues, advise businesses on corporate transactions or engage in tax controversies which are akin to litigation.

a. Tax attorneys enjoy: intellectual challenges; working alone; creative resolutions; saving clients thousands of dollars in tax liability; being considered to practice in an elite area.

b. Challenges that tax attorneys face: extremely deadline intensive; mentally exhausting; statutory-heavy work.

c. Tax attorneys work at: firms of all sizes; consulting firms like KPMG or Ernst & Young; in-house at private corporations or banks; federal agencies such as the Department of Treasury or Department of Justice: Tax Division; state tax authorities; non-profits advocating on behalf of low income tax payers; large public entities like hospitals or foundations; U.S. Tax Court, state tax courts, U.S. Court of Claims.

6. Labor & Employment: Traditional labor law involves the representation of employers in their management of a unionized workforce or workforce that wants to become unionized. It involves the negotiation of collective bargaining, elections, grievance arbitrations, and unfair labor practice charges at the National Labor Relations Board. Employment law covers the rest of legal issues that employers encounter, including wage issues, executive compensation, discrimination/harassment, restrictive covenants such as non-solicitations/non-competes, ERISA, executive compensation and other issues relating to how a company hires, fires, disciplines and manages its workforce. This practice area typically has counseling and litigation components to it.

a. Labor & employment attorneys enjoy: counseling clients to make fair decisions for their employees; using psychological and relational perspectives to address and resolve employee complaints; learning the intricacies of businesses and their operations, information, competitors, and workforce.

b. Challenges that labor & employment attorneys face: difficult, overlapping federal, state and local laws to consider; emotionally-charged situations; counterintuitive, employee-friendly laws.

c. Labor & employment attorneys work at: law firms of all sizes; in-house usually at companies with larger or unionized workforces; federal agencies such as NLRB, DOL, OSHA, EEOC or DOT; state labor boards and human rights agencies; city law departments; public interest organizations that litigate and lobby for employee rights; hospital in-house counsels; labor unions; administrative law judges.

7. Insurance: Insurance coverage attorneys review facts underlying an insurance claim and interpret policies to advise on whether the claim is covered under a particular insurance policy, such as home owners, renters, general liability, directors & officers, auto or employer's policies. Insurance defense attorneys are hired by insurance companies to represent their insureds in litigations involving claims against them. These claims are typically litigated in state and federal court and the subject matter of the lawsuit depends on the type of policy, *i.e.*, general liability policies typically involve slip & fall lawsuits, employer policies involve claims of harassment, discrimination or breach of employment contracts, etc.

a. Insurance attorneys enjoy: intellectual challenge of untangling complicated contract language in insurance policies; opportunities for high-volume litigation experience; opportunity to focus in specific types of litigation matters; recession-proof business; insurance companies are stable clients.

b. Challenges that insurance attorneys face: tiresome process of sifting through and interpreting lengthy, complicated contracts when doing insurance coverage work; insurance companies can be picky in paying legal bills for insurance defense work; some types of insurance claims (especially personal injury or car accident) can involve gruesome or disturbing circumstances.

c. Insurance attorneys work at: law firms of all sizes; in-house at insurance companies or large companies that purchase insurance; federal agencies like the FDIC, DOT, PBGC, State Departments of Insurance or Finance; hospitals; health care organizations; clerks or judges at all levels.

8. Administrative: These attorneys represent companies before the FCC, FTC, FDA, Consumer Product Safety Commission and other federal and state regulatory agencies. This type of regulatory work is concentrated mostly in the Washington, D.C, area and typically involves some sort of underlying constitutional challenge being made or defended by the business. This practice has both litigation and transactional components to it.

a. Administrative attorneys enjoy: operating within an inner circle of influence, the overlapping issues that touch on both government and business; job security.

b. Challenges that administrative attorneys face: dealing with slow-moving government agencies, feeling like their work is not creative; political hierarchy.

c. Administrative attorneys work at: law firms with government practice groups; in-house at companies that have regulatory matters (environmental, communications, health issues, etc.); virtually all federal and state agencies; large NGOs such as Sierra Club or Human Rights Watch; unions, interest groups; clerks and judges on all levels.

9. Family: These attorneys represent individual clients on legal matters impacting families including divorce, paternity, prenuptial and post-nuptial agreements, guardianship matters, adoption, child support and child custody and often advise on estate or tax-related issues. Historically, family law matters were primarily resolved through litigation but there have been movements towards achieving resolution through more collaborative approaches.

a. Family law attorneys enjoy: mediating and collaborating with parents to achieve children's best interests; developing close interpersonal relationships with clients and counseling clients on personal matters; formulating legal arguments which are typically more fact-based rather than based on legal precedent.

b. Challenges that family law attorneys face: highly-emotional issues causing clients to act unreasonably; congested court systems; acrimonious matters involving domestic abuse and suffering children.

c. Family law attorneys work at: small, boutique law firms; federal agencies such as Department of Health and Human Services, Administration for Children and Families; state departments of human, social and/or family services and related agencies; public guardian offices; non-profit organizations dealing with divorce, child custody, adoption, and domestic abuse; state court systems which usually have special family court branches.

10. Energy: This practice deals with issues that businesses face in the oil & gas industries, electricity and new energy like solar and wind. Energy attorneys protect their clients' rights as they explore, produce, acquire/sell property and minerals and help them navigate the various environment issues they can encounter along the way. Energy attorneys often negotiate documents, conduct diligence and deal with geological or logistical issues.

a. Energy attorneys enjoy: the ability to work in-house and earn highly-profitable stock options; intellectual challenges of dealing with tangible assets and complicated financial issues; being part of a highly-relevant, recession-proof industry.

b. Challenges that energy attorneys face: the industry is highly consolidated so there are few potential clients; balancing profitability concerns with environmental issues can be challenging.

c. Energy attorneys work at: law firms of all sizes; in-house at energy companies; federal agencies such as the Department of Energy, Department of Interior, U.S. Geological Survey, Department of Justice: Anti-trust Division or DOT; state AG's offices or departments of energy; NGO's like the National Wildlife Federation; clerks and judges at all levels.

11. Environmental: This practice area is split between private attorneys defending/counseling businesses versus public interest groups lobbying/litigating to protect and preserve the environment. Private practice environmental attorneys can advise real estate developers and municipalities regarding issues relating to restoration/remediation, air, water and waste disposal. Environmental attorneys also spend their time prosecuting/defending large class action lawsuits or government investigations involving these issues.

a. Environmental attorneys enjoy: being charged with the responsibility of protecting the environment; keeping private businesses profitable despite expensive and invasive regulations; advising profit-driven businesses to do right by the environment.

b. Challenges that environmental attorneys face: the good guy/bad guy dichotomy among public and private attorneys in this area; the enormous, document-intensive litigations/investigations that can drag on for tens of years; public interest positions have low compensation.

c. Environmental attorneys work at: law firms of all sizes; in-house at large real estate developers or businesses that have environmental issues (oil & gas, manufacturers, etc.); federal agencies such as EPA, Department of Energy, DOL, Department of Defense, Department of Justice: Environmental and Natural Resources Division; state agencies like Department of Environmental Quality or state-equivalents of EPA; local government branches; non-profit organizations like Earthjustice; clerks and judges of all levels.

12. Entertainment: This practice area involves representing artists, athletes, studios, directors, distributors, financiers, or other individuals or entities involved in the entertainment industry. These attorneys draft and negotiate agreements dealing with various legal issues such as intellectual property, publicity, employment, financing or ownership rights. Entertainment attorneys who represent artists can function as an agent and sometimes encounter labor law issues. This practice area is largely focused in New York and Los Angeles.

a. Entertainment attorneys enjoy: the publicity associated with working with celebrities; being around talented individuals; the dual, more personal role of acting as an agent and attorney.

b. Challenges that entertainment attorneys face: dealing the egos of talented artists, athletes or large studios; simplicity of the practice area; competitive practice difficult to break into; sometimes feels more like managing personalities than providing legal services.

c. Entertainment attorneys work at: law firms of all sizes; in-house at film studios, talent agencies, television stations, magazines, newspapers, venues and museums; federal agencies such as the FCC; state agencies such as the department of cultural affairs; non-profit organizations like the ACLU that advocate for free speech; labor unions; NCAA compliance office; judges, clerks and staff attorneys at federal courts.

13. Intellectual Property: This practice area breaks down into patents, trademarks and copyrights. Patent work is considered "hard IP" because one must have a "hard science" background to sit for the patent bar, such as engineering, biology or chemistry. IP law attorneys can also practice in copyright/trademarks, which are considered "soft IP." IP attorneys negotiate licensing agreements, litigate patent/copyright/trademark issues in federal court or file applications with the government for intellectual property rights. IP attorneys frequently work with new technologies, products and businesses in various industries.

a. Intellectual Property attorneys enjoy: the excitement of being on the cutting edge of new technologies; the elite status of the practice area; working with talented artists or brilliant inventors; the intellectual challenge of meshing science and law.

b. Challenges that intellectual property attorneys face: solitary work; quick deadlines for licensing work; dealing with ego-centric clients; difficult to break into this practice area without passing the patent bar.

c. Intellectual Property attorneys work at: law firms of all sizes; in-house at any company that is creating new brands, technology or entertainment; federal agencies such as the Department of Commerce and the United States Patent and Trademark Office, U.S. Army Corp. of Engineers, NASA or the Department of Energy; non-profit organizations or charities that engage in public policy efforts in issues of technology, internet or free speech, such as the ACLU; federal courts with specialized IP divisions.

14. Immigration: This practice area is split between business immigration and deportation work. Business immigration attorneys help individuals gain citizenship or work visas through employment in the United States. These attorneys also help individuals gain their path to citizenship through marriage to an American citizen. Deportation immigration attorneys represent individuals under threat of being deported or seeking asylum. Immigration work is governed exclusively by federal regulation.

a. Immigration attorneys enjoy: the feeling of reuniting clients with their families; client exposure; helping American-based companies recruit talent worldwide; recurring work from clients with large workforces; few deadlines.

b. Challenges that immigration attorneys face: dealing with slow-moving government agencies; routine, lengthy paperwork; isolating work; deportation work can be emotionally-charged.

c. Immigration attorneys work at: law firms of all sizes; in-house at companies with a large international workforce; federal agencies such as the USCIS, Department of Justice: Civil Rights Division, Department of Homeland Security: ICE, Customs Border Control, immigrant rights non-profit organizations; judges, clerks and staff attorneys at immigration courts and federal appellate courts.

15. Criminal: Criminal lawyers represent defendants in the criminal court system. They prepare for and appear at arraignments, pretrial hearings, settlement conferences, trials and sentencing hearings. They investigate and compile eye witness testimonies, police reports, and various other types of evidence pertinent to a particular case and they use this evidence, along with their knowledge of penal and constitutional laws, to defend adults and juveniles in federal, state and local tribunals. A criminal lawyer's constant adversary is the government.

a. Criminal attorneys enjoy: close relationships with their clients; defending and protecting an individual's civil liberties; small community of practitioners; crisis management.

b. Challenges that criminal attorneys face: dealing with defending a guilty client; overwhelming workload and high stress, especially during trials; getting paid by indigent clients.

c. Criminal attorneys work at: federal, state and city public defenders' offices, legal aid organizations; prosecutor's office, Department of Justice, city attorney's office, SEC, JAG Corp., AG's office, firms of all sizes.

16. Civil/Commercial Litigation: Litigation is any dispute between two or more parties that is placed before some kind of tribunal — such as federal, state, city or county court, arbitrator or specialized administrative agency. There are general litigators, who are retained for their expertise in adversarial practice, knowledge of procedure and experience with drafting, arguing motions and/or conducting trials. Other litigators can focus in particular areas like appellate work, product liability, toxic tort, securities, or antitrust.

a. Litigators enjoy: constantly learning new industries, practice areas or types of disputes; the thrill of victory and the satisfaction of defeating your adversary; persuading judges; protecting unjustly accused defendants.

b. Challenges that litigators face: being viewed as an unwanted expense by clients; clogged court systems; highly unpredictable, deadline-driven schedule; difficult to generate clientele or market your services without a practice area focus; unpleasant interactions with adversaries; cases can drag on for many years;

c. Litigators work at: law firms of all sizes; in-house at large companies that are constantly engaged in litigation; judges, clerks and staff attorneys at courts of all levels.

One extra note about litigation: law students should be particularly cautious about pursuing general litigation. Litigation is the most common attorney job offered to law students after graduation because first-year litigation associates primarily assist with legal research and drafting memoranda — two skills that are relatively strong coming out of law school. However, recent graduates can quickly become pigeon-holed in litigation before they realize it is not a good fit for them and have serious difficulty transitioning to a different practice area.

If you struggle with public speaking, are not a competitive person, have difficulty with dispute resolution or working under tight deadlines, get emotionally upset or become distracted from negative interactions with others or have little patience for an unpredictable work schedule, then you may be dissatisfied with a career as a litigator.

Other Practice Areas

Here is a list of other practice areas within the legal industry that may be worth exploring:

Admiralty	Construction	Agriculture
Antitrust	Aviation	Banking
Civil Rights	Communications	White Collar Crime
Fashion	Foreclosure	Franchising
Healthcare	Hospitality	Internet
Privacy	Legal Malpractice	Mass Tort
Advertising	Special Education	Personal Injury
Products Liability	Retail	Securities Fraud
Education	Workers Compensation	Exporting/Importing

Industries

Some practice areas are defined by their industry, such as real estate, entertainment, energy. Others, however, can be even further narrowed within a particular industry. For example, a corporate lawyer can focus only in representing individuals and businesses in the financial services industry. Employment lawyers can focus only in the professional services or labor lawyers can specialize in the real estate management industry. Or patent attorneys can focus in the biotechnology industry. This is just one additional layer of analysis when honing in your search to the career that best suits you.

PART II:

GETTING YOUR INTERNSHIP

Using the information and insights developed through Part I, now focus your energy on obtaining a legal internship that forges the path to achieving your career goals. It is time to design and execute an action plan to get the job that is best for you. Part II walks through finding, applying, and interviewing for internship opportunities and how to achieve successful results at each step.

Chapter 3

FINDING INTERNSHIP OPPORTUNITIES

The first step in the application process is searching for potential opportunities. Your search for internships should be targeted, but your efforts should be multi-dimensional. In other words, you should not be searching indiscriminately for any opportunity, but rather only those positions that would further your career goals.

Once you are able to articulate this desired position (or type of position), you should then be working diligently to leverage and expand your network, explore job postings online and in print publications and even try to create a new internship opportunity in that area. This strategy will give you the best chance of uncovering the highest quantity and quality of opportunities out there for you.

Intelligently Narrow Your Job Search

Before launching into your search, identify your target internship. This is important. While it may feel awkward to disregard a paying position at a reputable organization when you have no other apparent opportunities, keep your eyes on the prize. Without clear direction, you risk being distracted and/or wasting valuable time searching for internships that are misaligned with your career goals or patently unattainable. A focused job search will maximize the return on your time.

Always remember — your time is finite. Searching for the wrong position today may mean missing out on the right opportunity tomorrow.

> Side Note: Keep in mind that, in the fortunate circumstance that you are offered an interview, an interviewer may sometimes ask: "Where else have you applied?" If your applications are all over the place, this fact may hurt your credibility and make you appear unfocused, uncommitted or disingenuous.

There are two categories of internships for which you should search: Direct Internships and Stepping Stone Internships. Your current qualifications will dictate which category you should spend the majority of your time pursuing.

Direct Internships are internships that would make you most qualified to obtain your first attorney job. In other words, Direct Internships share the same practice area, location and organization type as the attorney position that you want to land upon graduation. For example, if it is your goal to be hired as an associate attorney at a mid-sized law firm in Chicago practicing real estate law, then a Direct Internship would be any internship where you work in real estate at a private law firm located in

Chicago. Plain and simple, if you are qualified, Direct Internships are the first choice.

However, you may be partially qualified or not qualified at all for a Direct Internship. If that is the case, then you should be allocating part or all of your search efforts trying to find Stepping Stone internships. These are internships in the same practice area as your desired attorney position, but with one or more different characteristics, such as location, organization type, sector or clientele. As the name indicates, these Stepping Stone Internships present the opportunity to obtain the qualifications needed to get hired for a Direct Internship in your next application cycle. They are a strategic way to get the job you want down the road.

For example, if you are not qualified to get hired for a real estate internship at a firm in Chicago, consider whether you *are* qualified for an internship at:

- A housing court judge in Chicago;
- A Chicago non-profit specializing in representing indigent clients in housing matters;
- A real estate firm in Detroit;
- The Federal Housing Administration; or
- The Chicago Housing Authority.

Any one of these Stepping Stone Internships would make you qualified for a Direct Internship, help build your network within the relevant community of professionals, potentially find a mentor and demonstrate your interest in the relevant practice area.

You should honestly assess whether, based on your qualifications, your time is best spent searching for Direct Internships or Stepping Stone Internships before moving forward. Once you narrow down the type(s) of internships you want to obtain, it is time to start your search.

> *What are your career goals? Based on those goals, what is the first attorney job you want to have after you graduate? Based on that job, what would be a Direct Internship? What credentials would your Direct Internship require? Do you have these credentials? If not, what are some Stepping Stone Internships that will enable you to obtain the required credentials and apply in the future?*

Discover Opportunities Through Your Network

Aside from your actual abilities, the next most powerful professional tool is your network. Virtually all of your career goals are made possible in one way or another through your relationships. Therefore, the earlier you devote energy towards maintaining, expanding and utilizing your network, the more stability, mobility, security and prosperity you will have in your career. It really is about "who you know."

This principle rings especially true during your search for internships. Utilizing and expanding your existing network will likely lead to the discovery of internship opportunities. The people within your network have their own information and relationships, either of which may open a new door to an internship. In addition, there may be people in your network who have the ability to hire you or recommend that you be hired.

Think of your network as a garden. Growing in your garden are all of your current relationships. Some relationships may be blossoming. Others may be young and barely budding or older and starting to wilt. No matter what, you should always be watering and shining light on your relationships while planting new seeds for the future. In your search for internship opportunities, relying upon your network may be quite fruitful. That is why networking at this stage is so important.

Identifying your Network

Even before you start attempting to grow your network, you should survey exactly who is currently in your professional network. Generally speaking, an individual is part of your network if they share some commonality with you that makes them more likely to respond to your email or telephone call.

You may be very close with someone in your network. Or you may not have ever spoken with them at all. Regardless, their potential responsiveness to your telephone call/email is an asset. And if they possess knowledge or relationships that may be of value to you, there is no reason why you should delay in starting a dialogue with them to maintain or develop the relationship.

There are two kinds of people who make up your network — your contacts and weak contacts. Your contacts are individuals who are members of the same formal or informal groups as you. The commonality with these people may be shared interests, origins, social circles, institutions or employment experiences. Examples of your contacts are people who:

- Live in your neighborhood;
- Went to the same school(s) as you;
- Enjoy the same recreational activities as you;
- Worked at same company as you;
- Are members of the same associations as you;
- Are fans of the same sports team(s) as you;
- Are members of the same religious congregation as you;
- Grew up in the same hometown as you;
- Work out in the same fitness club as you;
- Were in the same fraternity/sorority as you;
- Enjoy the same music or entertainment as you; or
- Are your friends and family.

Each of these groups creates a circle of people around you:

<u>YOUR NETWORK</u>

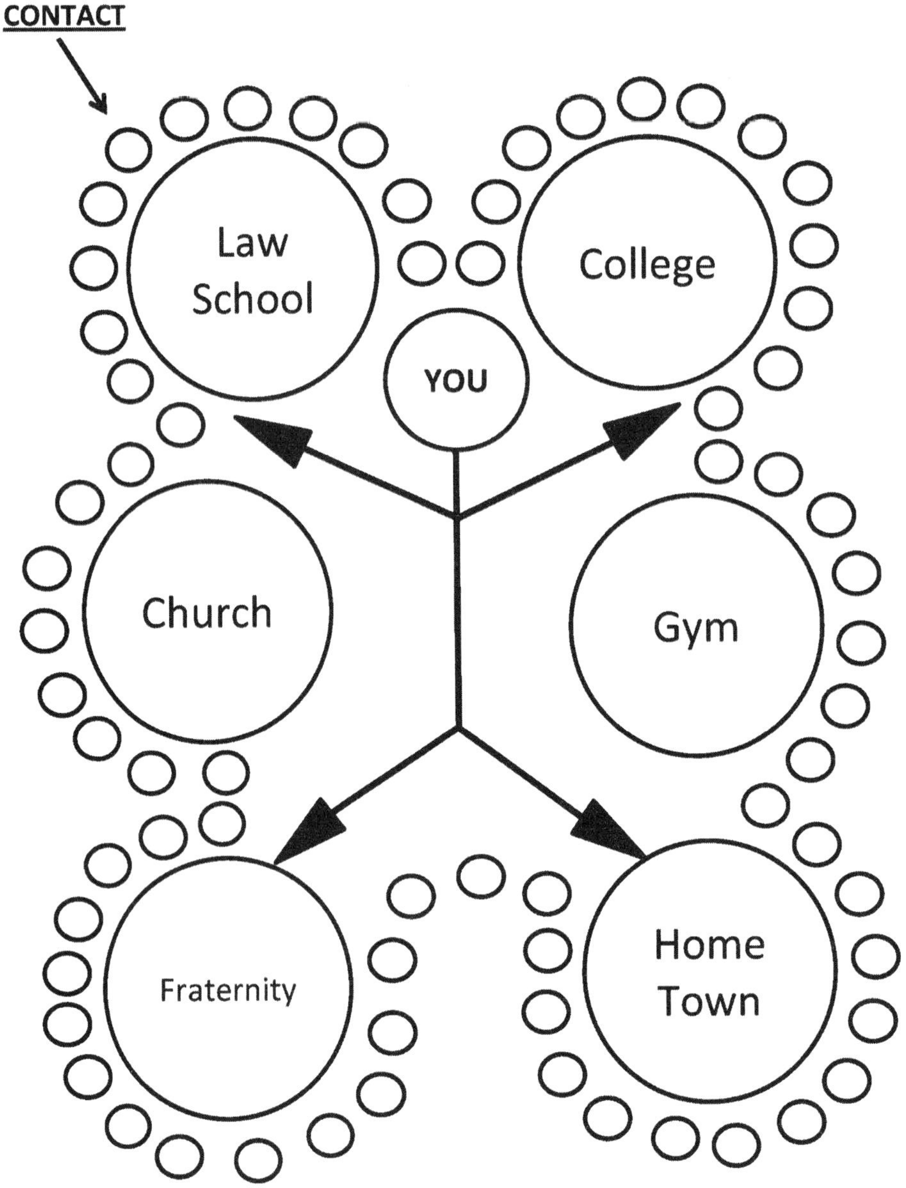

Any of the people surrounding you may be a prospective professional contact for you. They could be your future employer, employee, referral source, client or mentor. Or they may eventually introduce you to someone who will play one of these highly beneficial roles in your career.

Who is in your network? Do you know what these people do for a living? Do they possess any information that could be valuable to you? Have they undergone any experiences that are relevant to your career path? Do they know people that you would like to meet for these same reasons?

Your weak contacts may be some of the most valuable people in your career. You should be curious about who they are and finding ways to meet them. Weak contacts are the people within your contacts' network. Thus, your commonality with these people is your shared relationship with someone. Your weak contacts' circles connect with your circles though a person or multiple people:

YOUR CONTACT'S NETWORK

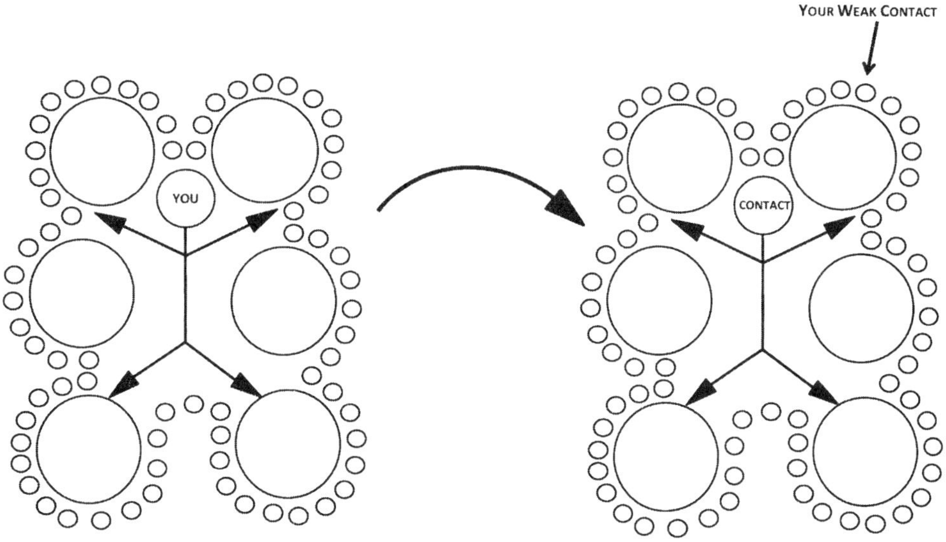

The strength of your connection to a weak contact is a sliding scale depending on the closeness of each of you to your shared contact. For example, your brother's longtime business partner may technically be your weak contact, but you may both be so close to your brother that the partner is almost certain to be responsive. Other weak contacts, on the other hand, may be so attenuated that a response is unlikely.

Regardless, your weak contacts are always just one step away from an in-person meeting. They may attend the same networking events and social events as you. They are also visible on social media. If you see an open door to initiating a dialogue with a weak contact who may be helpful to you in your career, you should walk through it. Opening up your networking efforts to your weak contacts, along with your contacts, will create exponentially more opportunities for you.

Linkedin may be the best place to seek out weak contacts. Review your "second connections" on Linkedin and look for people who may possess valuable information or relationships. Then write your shared connection an email asking for an introduction or blessing to reach out to the weak contact:

Hi Chris —

I was looking through Linkedin and noticed that you are connected to Susan Moshe. How well do you know her? I ask because she works at ABC Co., and that is a company that I am hoping to join after graduation.

Would you be comfortable if I messaged her directly, told her that you and me are friends, and asked her to get lunch sometime? A meeting with her would be incredibly valuable for me at this point in my career.

Best,

Lori

Emails like this can potentially lead to long-lasting, beneficial relationships. Sometimes people don't respond. Sometimes people respond with a "no, thank you." But you never know what will happen unless you put yourself out there. And if they do respond positively, then reach out to the weak contact to ask for an informational interview, as discussed below.

> *Who is in your network? What formal groups do you belong to? What informal groups? Who are your direct contacts? Who are your weak contacts? Do any of these people have knowledge or relationships that may be valuable to you? When was the last time you communicated with them? Would they respond if you emailed them? Do you think you have a strong network? If not, are you doing anything to change that?*

Networking Events

Regardless of the strength of your network, you should never stop trying to expand it. To do that, you must get out there in the world and meet people and the most popular way to meet people during law school is to attend a "networking event."

Networking events typically center on a professional group, topic or cause and allot time for attendees to mingle. Knowing how to navigate and maximize the value of these events will enable you to efficiently expand your network. And as you do, you will inevitably gain exposure to more opportunities, including internship opportunities.

First, you must see these events for what they really are — that is, an opportunity to get some brief face time with someone who shares a common interest and, by virtue of their attending the event also, has demonstrated openness to meeting new people. That is all. Networking events are not the time to ask for favors, connect deeply with someone, get drunk and have some laughs, share your life story or impress with your legal knowledge or expertise. Rather, it is simply a time to plant seeds for the future.

Effective use of a networking event is a three-step process:

Step 1: Research. Before the networking event, research the topic/cause, recent trends, changes, news or anything else relevant to the reason why people are congregating. Do your best to be a well-informed attendee with the ability to spark and lead a conversation. Also, to the extent possible, research who else will be attending the event. Research the speakers, panelists, hosts and/or attendees. Try to know beforehand which attendees may be a good contact for you and prepare conversation topics for when you have the opportunity to speak with them.

Step 2: Connect. While at the networking event, introduce yourself and engage in conversations with different people. Be the first to say "hello." Be open, engaging but not over-eager. Try not to get locked into one conversation the entire time. But also don't float around like a politician. The goal should be to connect with people (hopefully valuable contacts) about substantive, professional topics. Be yourself. Be personable. Be a good listener. Try to open the door to future interactions. Ask them for their business card/contact information so you can control the follow up after the event.

Step 3: Follow up. If you connect with someone in a positive way, you have now added a new contact to your network. This is just the beginning. Make sure to water that seed by following up and asking for an informational interview — *the most effective networking tool.*

> Side note: Any time that you venture outside of your home, you are putting yourself in a position to meet new people and expand your network. Your commute, class, barbeques, bars, parties, sporting events or other social gatherings typically involve introductions to new people. Don't be afraid to talk about your career or ask others about theirs. You may end up converting a social connection into a professional one.

Informational Interviews

An "informational interview" ("II") is a blanket term for any one-on-one meeting with an individual within your network where the purpose is for you to ask them questions. In the most general sense, an II is a proposition for another professional to sit down and let you pick their brain about a particular topic. For all law students, especially ones on the hunt for an internship, the topic of the II should always be a particular sector, organization, practice area, industry or other topics related to the interviewee's career and your potential career path.

Despite what the name suggests, II's need not be formal. For convenience, they typically take place at someone's office or conference room during business hours. But they can also be conducted over coffee, breakfast, lunch, dinner or drinks. Although in-person II is most preferable, it can be done telephonically as well.

Regardless of whether you are maintaining or strengthening an existing relationship with a contact or developing a new relationship with a weak contact, an II is the time to shine. You need to learn how to obtain and conduct an II in order to gather valuable information, make a positive impression, obtain introductions to new people and meaningfully connect with another professional in your field.

Email Request for an Informational Interview

Your initial email to a potential interviewee must make clear that they can help your career simply by showing up and answering questions off the top of their head. It must not seem like you will ask them for a favor or that they should prepare beforehand — which are common reasons why someone would decline or simply not respond to your request for an II.

In addition, your email should be concise, well-written, error-free and in an appropriate tone. The interviewee will be more willing to spend their time with someone whom they view as professional and polished.

When you identify a potential interviewee, write them an email explaining who you are, how you came to reach out to them and ask if they would be open to meeting with you. Here are some example emails:

Email to someone you met at networking event:

Dear Mr. Jackson:

You and I met at the criminal law symposium last week. I truly enjoyed our brief conversation about the mistreatment of POWs abroad and appreciated your insights on how to improve conditions.

As I mentioned, I am considering a career in prisoners' rights and actively trying to obtain as much information as possible about this field of practice.

Would you be willing to meet with me to discuss your career path and thoughts on the practice generally? Any insight you might be able to share would be incredibly valuable for me at this stage in my legal career. I will make myself available at your convenience.

Either way, I hope all is well with you.

Sincerely,

Chris Anderson

Email to a family friend:

Dear Matt:

My sister recently mentioned to me that you work as an attorney for the National Labor Relations Board in Washington, DC. I'm not sure if you knew, but I am in my second year of law school and have been considering pursuing a career in labor law. I'm currently taking Labor Law II and really enjoy it.

Would you be open to meeting with me so I could ask you some questions about your career? I am curious to learn of the differences between the study of labor law and actually practicing it. Other than classes on Mondays and Wednesdays, my schedule is wide open. I would be happy to come to your office or anywhere else that would be convenient for you.

Best,

Lindsey

Email to a weak contact through a professor:

Dear Mr. Gonzalez:

My professor, Timothy Shragin, suggested that I reach out to you. I am currently a first-year law student at Pace Law School pursuing a career in real estate litigation and trying to obtain information about whether this would be a good fit for me in my career.

Would you be willing to meet with me briefly so I can ask you a few questions about practicing real estate litigation? Any insight you might have would be much appreciated. Please just let me know whatever date and time work for you and I'll make myself available.

Thank you so much,

Susan Hennelly

These examples are meant to be used as a reference, not a template. Your email to a potential interviewee must be tailored to the specific circumstances and relationship. Here are a few important things to keep in mind when emailing a potential interviewee:

1. **They may never respond to your email.** Or, they may respond to the first email, but then go dark after that. Do not take this personally. There are myriad reasons why someone may be non-responsive. Stay positive and give them the benefit of the doubt. The only way to spark new relationships is to be vulnerable and put yourself out there. And, to put yourself out there, you must develop a thick skin.
2. **Make yourself available.** If they do respond, unless completely impractical, make sure to accommodate whatever date, time and location works for them. Do not make scheduling an issue unless absolutely necessary.
3. **Mirror the tone of their emails.** As you are scheduling the II, if the interviewee continues to write to you in a formal manner, make sure to keep your emails formal as well. You must maintain your positive first impression throughout your email exchange.

Conducting an Informational Interview

Regardless of where it takes place, approach each II with subtle professionalism. Research your interviewee beforehand, arrive early, dress formally and bring a notepad and pen. Thank the interviewee for taking the time to meet with you and be prepared to lead the interview with a list of questions. The interviewee should need to do nothing other than sit back and answer questions. They should feel comfortable, relaxed, important and interesting. If they dictate the flow of conversation, then follow their lead but keep your questions in mind.

Your questions should have dual purposes. First and foremost, they should gather the necessary information to enable you to make a well-informed career choice. Second, the substance of the questions should make a positive impression upon the interviewee by implicitly conveying the message that you are serious, personable, well-prepared, interested in their field, intelligent, respectful of their time and thoughtful. You want to come off as their potential colleague someday.

Here are some sample lines of questioning for an II:

- *What is your job like? What do you do? What are your duties/functions? What kind of problems do you deal with? What kinds of decisions do you make? What percentage of your time is devoted to what?*
- *Why did this type of work interest you? What drew you to this practice area? Organization? Location? Industry?*
- *How did you obtain your current position? What was your path?*
- *What do you enjoy most about your job? What do you dislike the most? What do you find most satisfying? What is most challenging? Most stressful? What do you like/dislike about the particular practice area? Organization? Location? Industry?*
- *Can you describe your work environment? Busy, hectic or calm? Is it a competitive atmosphere? Collaborative? What can you tell me about the corporate culture?*
- *How does your job impact your lifestyle? Do you have flexibility in your schedule? Work weekends? Are there organizations that you are expected to join? What are the salary ranges in your field? Is there a ceiling?*
- *How is the economy affecting your organization? Practice area? Industry? What is the overall outlook in your field? Demand for new attorneys?*
- *How can a law student obtain the necessary experience to get a position like yours? What is your organization (or organizations like yours) looking for in a candidate? Where might I meet people in your field? Knowing what you do about my background (education, GPA, work experience, achievements), do you think I have the requisite credentials to obtain an internship in your field? What do you suggest I do to improve my candidacy?*

Take notes of their answers. Do not scribble furiously to the point where it disrupts the flow of the conversation. Just jot down general impressions or specific names, addresses, telephone numbers or follow up reminders. If the II takes place over drinks or a meal, without making it awkward, insist on paying the bill. Stay as long as they are willing to stay. Be prepared to talk about yourself. Bring a resumé, but do not present it unless asked.

And be endearing. The Q&A will lead to acquiring new information — a highly valuable commodity at the early stages of your career. But, perhaps just as importantly, this exchange will (hopefully) lead to developing a personal connection.

If the interviewee likes you and is willing to vouch for you as a professional, they will naturally start thinking of ways to help you. This is a secondary benefit of the II that must not be overlooked. Without you asking, the interviewee may offer to introduce you to someone, look into an internship opening at their organization or somewhere else, or send you helpful information. Your need for this type of assistance is obvious and underlies the entire II. If they want to help you, they will.

Follow Up After Informational Interview

Make sure that you follow up via email within a day or two after the II. Thank them for their time, insight and willingness to share their thoughts with you. If you offered to follow up with them regarding something specific, be sure to reference that in the email.

Likewise, if they offered you some assistance, be sure to include that in the follow up email. But be careful — now you are asking them for a favor. They don't owe you anything. Thus, asking for something requires writing with the correct tone. Here's a sample email to help illustrate this point:

> *Dear Mr. Dougherty:*
>
> *Thank you so much for meeting with me yesterday. I really enjoyed speaking with you about practicing entertainment law in Los Angeles and found your insights on the industry incredibly valuable.*
>
> *Attached is that article I mentioned during our conversation regarding recent changes to the Screen Actors Guild collective bargaining agreement. I hope you find it interesting and helpful in your practice.*
>
> *Also, I also wanted to follow up to check if you were still comfortable connecting me with your colleague Andrew Spillman? From what you described, he sounds like a person from whom I could learn very much and I would definitely like to meet him.*
>
> *Either way, thank you again. I hope you have a great weekend.*
>
> *Best regards,*
>
> *Jeffrey Coughlin*

If they don't respond to your follow up email despite offering you some assistance, follow up with a brief telephone call one week later inquiring whether they received the email. There is nothing wrong with following up on their offer to help. Just be professional and polite.

Throughout law school, you should constantly be engaged in a cycle of seeking out, coordinating and conducting IIs. These interactions will present many opportunities, including potential internship positions.

Discover Opportunities Through Online Postings

Online postings are the most popular job search resource for law students. Students tend to prefer these websites because they can browse and apply for innumerable internship opportunities without leaving their desk. Here are a few things to know before searching for internship opportunities online:

1. Consider Competition Level vs. Strength of Your Application

While you may feel compelled to throw out a few long shot applications for dream positions, you should generally be spending your time applying for positions that you have a strong chance of obtaining. To evaluate which online posting is a good bet, consider the level of competition for the position and the strength of your application.

The competition for a position posted online is largely dictated by the website traffic and the attractiveness of the position. Websites that are highly-trafficked by law students naturally draw more applications. And positions that cover multiple practice areas, have higher compensation and/or are at reputable organizations will attract more candidates. These are the most common attributes that boost competition for a position posted online.

For instance, consider a high-paying general summer associate position at a large law firm posted on your law school's job/internship database. This is an attractive position posted on a website that is highly-trafficked by law students at your school and possibly other schools. The likelihood is that you will be competing with, at the least, the majority of the top-ranked students in your class and from other schools. Unless the credentials on your resumé match or exceed that which is required in the posting, don't apply. Your time is better spent on other endeavors such as continuing to search for other positions.

On the end of the spectrum, consider a posting for a bankruptcy clerk position in a law journal website with relatively small readership that offers less-than-market pay. The low pay makes this position less attractive, the bankruptcy requirement makes it inapplicable to many students without that type of focus and the low readership makes the posting less visible. For this position, your credentials need not perfectly match the required qualifications in order to get hired. Thus, if it furthers your best-suited career path and you can deal with the lower pay, then it would be a wise use of your time to apply for this position.

Chances are that most of the posted positions that you peruse will have a level of competition somewhere in between these examples. Assessing whether you should apply for a position online is an art, not a science. But just keep in mind that it is not necessarily quantity over quality; more applications does not equate to greater chances of getting hired. You should focus your energy applying for posted positions that strike the right balance between the level of competition and the strength of your qualifications.

2. Take Advantage of All Online Resources

There are likely more online resources for job postings than you think, and more are popping up frequently. In addition to your school's job database, include in your search organizations that post job openings on their own website, trade publications, online alumni newsletters, etc. The following table lists just a few websites that you should peruse during your search for an internship:

Type of Websites	Examples
General Job Aggregators	Monster.com, simplyhired.com, theladders.com, indeed.com, glassdoor.com, careerbuilder.com, linkedin.com, craigslist.org, internships.com, American's Job Bank, USPTO.gov, nalpdirectory.gov, abanet.org, nlg.org
Government Legal Job Aggregators	Usajobs.gov, usdoj.gov/oarm, Oscar.uscourts.gov, ncsconline.org, prosecutor.info
General Legal Job Aggregators	Lawjobs.com, lawmatch.com, lawcrossing.com, legalcareers.com, martindale.com, legalstaff.com, abovethelaw.com, ihirelegal.com, newlawyer.com, findlaw.com, attorneyjobs.com, counsel.net, emplawyer.com, careers.findlaw.com, lawforum.net, Complaw Attorney Job Listings, Building Better Legal Profession, Already Bored, hr.org, NAWL Career Center, chronicle.com, jobstick.com; vault.com
Environmental, Non-profit or Public Interest Legal Job Aggregators	aam-us.org, aclu.org, Advancementproject.org, idealist.org, pic.org, hrusa.org, ecomall.com, afi.org, palidan.com, envirolink.org, derechos.org

3. Don't Get Hung Up on the Job Title

Keep in mind that an opportunity does not need to be identified in a posting as an "internship" to be worthy of pursuit. As explained above, an internship is any job opportunity that permits you to gain practical experience in the legal field during law school. Thus, for your purposes, an internship opportunity may be posted as a position for a clerk, apprentice, fellow, extern, or even legal secretary or paralegal. If the practice area, organization, location, industry and other characteristics are aligned with your desired internship, then you may want to consider applying for the position and exploring the opportunity further.

> Side Note: Nothing prevents you from taking an interview for a paralegal position and asking whether they would be open to giving you attorney-related work in addition to the paralegal work. If an organization needs the help and trusts your work product, there is no reason why you shouldn't try to expand your role once you get your foot in the door. This angle is more likely to be successful at a smaller organization. If you elect this strategy, however, just be wary of being typecast in a paralegal role. Always keep your focus on performing attorney-related work.

Discover Opportunities Through Print Publications

Although it may seem outdated, there are still many great job opportunities posted in print publications. These are usually posted by less tech-savvy attorneys at smaller firms; and there are many of those types of attorneys out there.

The upside is that the readership of these print publications is likely a fraction of a typical website's online traffic and, therefore, the competition for these positions will likely be lower. Consider reviewing bar association publications, alumni newsletters or magazines, law journals or the job ads section in newspapers. You may find some gems in there.

Create Internship Opportunities

The last way to seek out internship opportunities is to create one. This requires research, creativity and salesmanship. But if you are successful in creating a new internship opportunity, then it is all yours with no competition at all.

First step to creating an internship is identifying the hidden and/or unrealized need for an intern. Organizations are constantly changing, expanding and/or contracting. Sometimes business is slow and a company may employ too many people with not enough work to go around. Other times, a company may be bursting at the seams and needs immediate extra staff. The key to creating an internship is sending a targeted, persuasive letter at the right time to an organization that is experiencing the latter.

Do some research. Start with google. Talk to people in your network. Read the newspaper and law journal. Poke around and survey the recent events in your desired internship location. Try to follow the breadcrumbs to an opportunity. Examples of such changes may include:

- A law firm recently obtaining a new client;
- A law firm recently appearing as counsel of record in a large lawsuit;
- A company expanding, merging, or acquiring another company;
- A non-profit receiving new grant money or launching a new initiative;
- The passing of legislation increasing the workload for an organization; or

- An organization that recently lost a key employee.

Any one of these organizations may have just acquired a need for an intern and they may not even know it yet. Once you identify their need, send a tailored cover letter (enclosing resumé) to a decision-maker at the organization. In it, explain the reason for their need for an intern and why your qualifications make you the right person to be that intern. Tell them what you can do for them and how you propose doing it.

Side Note: Smaller organizations, with less infrastructure or human resources personnel, will typically be more receptive to your proposal to create an internship.

Track Your Progress

While you engage some or all of these efforts to identify and search for internship opportunities, organize and track your progress. Create a spreadsheet with all potential leads with information such as the one on the next page.

As you attend networking events, conduct informational interviews, search for postings and try to create your own internships, plug all of the relevant information into your spreadsheet and refer back to it on a daily basis. This will help you launch a balanced attack and focus your energy in a diversified way. It will also ensure that no opportunity falls through the cracks due to neglect, unexplored avenues or missed deadlines.

Employer	Position	Details on Position	Relevant Contacts	Means of Discovery	Application Materials	Desired credentials	Application Deadline	Notes
San Francisco Attorney General's Office	Part-time law clerk	Assist with trial preparation; $15/hr; potential for full-time	Neighbors with legal secretary at AG's office	Posting on AG's website	Resumé, cover letter, writing sample, copy of transcript	Experience in litigation; bi-lingual a plus	January 15	Spoke with neighbor, need to follow up next week; started drafting cover letter; need to request transcript
Los Angeles District Attorney's Office	Full-time intern	Special document review project; $20/hr;	Linkedin weak contact with trial attorney at DA's office through friend	School website	Resumé and cover letter	Proficient in excel; ability to travel	January 30	Sent email to college friend asking for introduction to DA attorney weak contact; need to brush up on excel skills.

Chapter 4

APPLYING FOR INTERNSHIPS

Your materials submitted in application for an internship are your first, and possibly only, opportunity to make the right impression on the hiring organization. Without explicitly saying it, you should tell the reader that you are the perfect fit for the position. This message is best conveyed through a professional, clean-looking, well-written resumé and cover letter that together seamlessly present a compilation of experiences, achievements, skills, interests, and intentions that match the organization's needs. Your application must explain logically and persuasively why the organization should become the next chapter of your story.

YOUR RESUMÉ

The resumé anchors your entire application. This document is a living, breathing written work that adapts to become your best representation for a particular purpose. It is situationally-appropriate compilation of information. Your educational and employment experiences, skills, accomplishments and hobbies cannot all be adequately explained in a one-page document. Only those traits that would be meaningful under the circumstances should make the cut. Correctly deciding what stays and how it is described can make the difference between an interview offer and a rejection letter.

> Tip: It may be efficient to keep a resumé master list on your computer where you store any information you have included in prior versions of your resumé. Each time you apply, you can review and extract relevant information from your master list and tailor it to the specific position.

Identify What is Relevant

For resumé drafting, there is strong emphasis on the word "relevant." Relevant signifies information that is important, meaningful and attractive to a potential internship employer. Your resumé must be constructed, reorganized, reworded and revamped to highlight the most relevant information for the desired position. It should be tailored to fit each position. This requires some up-front research:

- **Study the job description posted.** Job descriptions are drafted with deliberateness and each desired qualification would not have been included unless it was important. To the extent possible, draft your resumé to match the job description.

- **Conduct an Informational Interview.** Meet with someone with relevant general or specific experience to find out what makes an internship candidate most attractive. Ask them questions to understand what really matters to the organization and what really happens in the workplace. A clearer understanding of the occupational realities will make you better equipped to draft a tailored resumé.
- **Conduct online research.** Read about the organization, practice area, industry, location, relevant recent news and trends. Glean from that information that might peak the organization's interest in your application.

> *Does your resumé contain qualifications that match the job description? Do you know what the organization is looking for in a candidate? Can you speak with someone who worked there? What have you done to find out what credentials might boost your chances of getting hired?*

THE CONTENT OF YOUR RESUMÉ

Every sentence should add value; if it does not, remove it. Specifically, each sentence of your resumé should fulfill one of the following three purposes:

1. Demonstrates that you are interested in relevant aspects of the position.

This is most persuasively accomplished through inclusion of prior legal work experience. Clearly, if you have worked with relevant clientele or in a relevant practice area, location or industry, then that work experience should be included. In addition, your non-legal work experience should be assessed and possibly included as well. For example, if you're applying for a real estate litigation internship, prior employment as a real estate broker demonstrates a relevant interest in the practice area.

Relevant interest can also be demonstrated through your elective coursework, memberships in clubs or associations, writing on journals, or even hobbies. For example, if you're applying for an internship at a public defender office and one of your hobbies is to volunteer at a soup kitchen, include that hobby. It would show your interests are aligned with the organization's — namely, providing a public service.

> Side Note — It is important to know when not to include a hobby. As example, international law firms don't care that you like to travel; sports law internship employers don't care that you played football in high school; and entertainment lawyers are not going to hire you because you love movies. Learning the difference between a relevant and non-relevant hobby can be difficult and is a ripe topic during an II with an attorney who has experience in your desired area/organization.

In sum, you should be thinking about who the organization works with and for, what type of problems they solve, where they perform their work, how they get their work done and why they do it (what motivates them). If your prior experience is connected in some way to their situation, then consider including it.

2. Demonstrates that you are intelligent and hard-working.

These traits are universally attractive to all potential internship employer irrespective of their field and are commonly demonstrated through achievement of high academic grades, rank, scholarships, awards and honors.

In addition, you can demonstrate your intelligence and work ethic in other less-conventionally ways. One way is through prior leadership roles. Have you ever been the captain of sports team, president of intramural club, ran a small business or venture or organized an event? These roles demonstrate that you are respected by your peers, have initiative, are organized, mature and responsible.

Another way is to highlight specific, quantifiable accomplishments at prior jobs (legal or non-legal). Have you assisted with litigation victories or closing a particular transactional deal, had an exceptional sales record at a company or received positive reviews from supervisors, offered a full-time position or promoted? These achievements add color to your work experiences and show that you were not just a person behind a desk but rather an active contributor to your prior employers.

3. Demonstrates that you are qualified for the position.

Your resumé should demonstrate that you are qualified by describing your relevant (a) general experience, (b) specific experience and/or (c) skills.

A candidate has relevant "general experience" if they previously worked in the same practice area, industry, location or with the same clientele as the internship organization. Along with demonstrating a relevant interest, these general experiences show that a candidate is familiar with the relevant cultural issues, organizational environment, professional community, problem-solving processes and legal issues that the internship organization faces.

A candidate has relevant "specific experience" if they have performed the same tasks as they will be performing at the internship organization. For example, relevant specific experience for internship in commercial litigation would be previously drafting pleadings, discovery demands, affidavits and motions, assisting with depositions, preparing trial exhibits, cite-checking, and filing documents with the court. Regardless of which organization the candidate worked for, they would be qualified for the internship position by virtue of this specific experience.

As a last resort, if you are unable to articulate prior relevant general or specific experience, you can nonetheless demonstrate that you are qualified through your relevant skills. Each internship position requires an intern to fulfill a particular role at the organization. Each particular role, in turn, involves the application of certain skills in order to accomplish the assigned tasks. Examples of skills include writing, researching, cite-checking, business generation, multitasking, fluency in multiple languages, working under pressure, proficiency with particular software or filing of documents. An employer may be willing to overlook lack of relevant experience if you have a strong and relevant skillset.

> *Are you submitting a resumé that is tailored specifically for the position you are seeking? Does each sentence add value? How? Is it clear from your resumé that you are interested in the relevant field? That you are intelligent and hard-working? That you are qualified for the position? Are there relevant experiences, accomplishments or other positive traits that you have not included in your resumé?*

Ten Resumé Drafting Tips

Because drafting a resumé is, by definition, a situationally-specific task, there are few principles that apply universally to all resumés. With that being said, here are a few tips to consider:

1. Limit it to one page. Absent extraordinary circumstances, your resumé should be one page. Accomplished professionals with numerous publications or client successes have two-page resumés. For the most part, a law student should be expected to fit their credentials on one page. A resumé longer than one page may mistakenly convey an undeserved, inflated sense of accomplishment that may be off-putting.

2. Important information should take up most space and appear at top. Resumés are read top to bottom and people lose interest quickly. Therefore, the most relevant information should be at the top of your resumé and then descend in order of importance. And remember to allocate space on your resumé according to importance. Your most recent legal work experience should always be a larger entry than your college coursework.

> Side Note: Make sure that the email address that you provide is professional. If you are still using your high school email address of kingdude99@hotmail.com or hottieclaire10@aol.com, stop it. These are unprofessional email addresses that may distort the professional image you are trying to craft. And continued use of an outdated email provider can show that you are not taking advantage or are unaware of new technology.

3. Be consistent with use of present/past tense. If you are currently participating in a particular activity or employed at an organization, you should write that entry in the present tense. Otherwise, write in past tense. Inadvertent inconsistencies in tense can be glaring for the reader.

4. Write work experience to flow logically. An entry describing a particular work experience should be structured in this order: name of organization, city/state of organization, date of employment, title, supervisors, clientele, industry, specific experience, example(s) of specific experience, skills and awards/achievements. Space is

always a consideration; not all of this information must be included. But this order should nonetheless be considered to ensure your information flows logically for the reader. Here are illustrations of this concept from each sector:

***Oak County District Attorney's Office**, Boston, MAMay 2013 – August 2013*

Full-time Law Clerk: Provided general assistance to trial attorneys in white collar criminal prosecutions. Conducted research and drafted legal memoranda on various criminal law-related topics such as search and seizure, Fifth Amendment, criminal rules of evidence, exculpatory evidence and attorney-client privilege. Drafted affidavits, complaints, charges, answers, proposed court orders, stipulations, confidentiality agreements and deposition outlines. Compiled exhibits and reviewed evidence to flag relevant issues. Following trial, drafted proposed court order to memorialize jury verdict that, after only minimal editing, was "so ordered" by the judge. Received "excellent" reviews from supervisors for organizational, research, writing skills, work ethic and personality. Offered an extension of full-time position for summer semester.

***Falkner Pratt & Dressler LLP**, New York, NY March 2014 – Present*

Part-time Legal Intern: Provide general assistance to intellectual property and entertainment practice groups in the representation of movie producers, actors, directors, financiers, theater owners and authors. Conduct legal research and draft memoranda on various topics including but not limited to copyright, trademark, formation of venture capital funds, publicity rights, federal and state securities regulations, federal court procedure and infringement. Draft royalty agreements, joint venture agreements, asset purchase agreements, cease and desist letters and talent agreements. Participated in the creation of a complex multi-entity fundraising venture in connection with the production of a Broadway play. Due to strong work performance, offered to increase work schedule from 10 to 20 hours per week.

***Creative Creations, Inc.**, Austin, TX November 2012 – February 2013*

Part-time Legal Extern: Worked directly for in-house general counsel at an interior design firm to provide legal services to the company in various areas such as employment, corporate, real estate, commercial litigation, bankruptcy and intellectual property. Conducted legal research and drafted internal memoranda, offer letters, employment agreements, termination letters, corporate charts, assignment/assumption agreements, leases, cease and desist letters, and the employee handbook. Reviewed, analyzed, compiled and delivered relevant documents to outside counsel in connection with the bankruptcy of a subsidiary and a commercial dispute with a vendor. Consistently received positive reviews from general counsel and management.

5. Expand your relevant "specific experiences." This is not a suggestion to be disingenuous. It is an acknowledgement that packing multiple months of work experiences into a single paragraph is difficult. It requires making tough decisions on what is most relevant and should be emphasized. As an illustration, consider the

paragraph above for "Creative Creations, Inc." Below is that same entry modified to apply for an internship in employment law:

> ***Creative Creations, Inc.**, Austin, TX* *November 2012– February 2013*
>
> *Part-time Legal Extern: Worked directly for in-house general counsel at an interior design firm to provide a variety of legal services to the company, particularly in the area of employment. Conducted legal research and drafted internal memoranda on topics such as age and race discrimination, harassment, wage and hour, constructive termination, reasonable accommodation and the Equal Pay Act. Drafted offer letters, employment agreements, termination letters, and multiple versions of the employee handbook. Took the lead on researching, drafting and implementing a new social media policy in multiple states. Consistently received positive reviews from general counsel and management regarding assistance rendered in addressing the legal issues relating to workforce.*

6. Use legal action verbs. The verbs used in your resumé are instrumental in attractively portraying your experience and abilities and should comport with those customarily used in the practice of law. You want to speak the reader's language — "legalese." Consider the following word choice comparisons:

Generic verbs	**Law practice-specific verbs**
Read	Review, analyze, examine
Find	Identify, locate, flag
Figure out	Assess, evaluate, determine, navigate
Write	Draft, transcribe, memorialize
Document	Contract, agreement, pleading, memoranda
Send	Transmit, submit, file
Put together	Compile, organize, categorize
Help	Assist, contribute, participate
Told	Advise, confer, communicate, correspond, report

7. Less relevant experience, more specificity. Your resumé should be no more than one page. But it should also be *no less* than one page. Empty space on a resumé screams lack of qualifications. Thus, if you can point to only a handful of assignments that are relevant to the position sought, then be sure to expand and describe those experiences in explicit detail. This will not only fill space and provide more relevant details, but also impress the reader by demonstrating your ability to clearly describe what you have done. As an illustration, consider the following sentence comparisons:

Condensed sentence	Expanded, detailed sentence
Reviewed contracts and informed supervising attorney about issues pertaining to real estate closing.	*Reviewed and analyzed assumption agreements, UCC-1s, mortgage term sheets and other transactional documents to identify factual and/or legal issues that could delay or prevent a commercial real estate closing in San Marino county.*
Researched legal issues regarding bankruptcy and drafted related court filings.	*Conducted legal research on the dischargeability of debts incurred by transacting with a sovereign nation and drafted attorney affirmation, client declaration, affidavit of service, and certification for submission to court.*

8. Use catchwords. Before your resumé is read thoroughly, it will likely be skimmed briefly. In that initial skim, you want special "catchwords" to grab the reader's attention and indicate that you are qualified. Some of these catchwords can be found in the job description for the position. Others may be the names of documents, statutes, procedures, court systems, or other terminology specific to a practice area or industry. Think of the catchwords that the reader of your resumé might be skimming for and do your best to include them. Here are some examples:

Position	Catchwords
Litigation Internship	Pleading, affidavit, affirmation, order, subpoena, declaration, court submission, memoranda of law, deposition, trial, exhibits, cite-checking, blue-booking, complaint, discovery, examination, argument.
Corporate Transactional Internship	Due diligence, document review, compliance, closing, private placement memoranda, prospectus, SEC, FINRA, securities regulation, merger/acquisition.
Labor & Employment Internship	Discrimination, harassment, wage and hour, labor union, representation, NLRB, NLRA, EEOC, human rights, termination, severance, organizing campaign, Title VII, ADA, FLSA, ERISA.
Bankruptcy Internship	Bankruptcy Code, Rules of Bankruptcy Procedure, discharge, petition, abandon, debtor, creditor, Chapter 7, 11 or 13, automatic stay, secured, unsecured, reorganization.

Position	Catchwords
Real Estate Internship	Closing, landlord/tenant, condominium, foreclosure, construction, lease, land use, refinance, mortgage, FHA, HUD, RESPA, short sale, deed, title search.
Criminal Law Internship	Criminal procedure, rules of evidence, penal code, prisoner, immunity, search and seizure, guilty, innocent, plea bargain, white collar, prosecutor, violation, investigation.
Immigration Law Internship	Foreign national, PERM, EB-1, H-1B, L-1, O, P, J-1 waivers, permanent resident, temporary visa, alien, USCIS, naturalization, INA, moral turpitude, asylum, undocumented, ICE.

9. No errors. Your resumé must be grammatically and spatially flawless. There are many stylistic decisions that you can make where there is no "right" way to do it. But, if you are inconsistent stylistically, then you are making errors. Critical readers will reflexively discard resumés containing mistakes in order to efficiently narrow the applicant pool. As a demonstration of how these "gremlins" can creep into your resumé, carefully review the following resumé excerpt for errors:

University of Denver, Sturm College of Law, Denver, CO
Candidate for Juris Doctorate, expected May 2015

Rank: 21 out of 235 [top 10%]
Honors: Marshall Brennan Scholarship for outstanding academic achievement

LEGAL WORK EXPERIENCE

Mark E. Povlosky, PLLC, Cambridge, MA January 2012-May 2013

Part-time Law Clerk: Assisted solo practitioner in representation of immigrant community by providing legal services in the areas of immigration law, personal injury, and criminal defense law. Conducted client intakes, answered telephones and generally managed office. Conduct legal research and drafted memoranda on various legal topics including but not limited to asylum, medical experts, rules of evidence in State and federal court and H-1B visas. Corresponded with USCIS and ICE to locate detained family members of clients.

Hifton Marfin Company, Boston, MA February 2011 – August 2011

Part-Time Legal Intern: Worked for associate general counsel for publishing company in the areas of intellectual property and corporate law. Conducted legal research and drafted internal memoranda on various topics including but not limited to privacy rights, use of likeness, modification of royalty agreements, fair use doctrine, copyright infringement and valuation of trademarks. Compiled 50-state survey on laws relating to sweepstakes. Drafted cease and desist letters and researched trademarks on the USPTO.

Can you spot the errors? There are eleven.

- The bolding of commas is inconsistent. The commas after "College of Law" and "Company" are all bold. But the comma after "PLLC" is not.
- The underlining of colons is inconsistent. The colon after "Rank," "Clerk" and "Intern" are all underlined. But the colon after "Honors" is not.
- Juris Doctorate is not the appropriate way to list your JD on your resumé. It should be expressed as either "Juris Doctor" or "Doctor of Jurisprudence."
- There should be a "the" before "representation."
- "Conduct" should be written in past tense.
- "State" has initial capitalization but "federal" does not.
- "Part-time Legal Intern" is erroneously indented by a single space.
- The word "part-time" is written two different ways. Once it has "time" with initial capitalization, the other it does not.
- The Oxford Comma is used in one instance, and not in another. Specifically, there is an Oxford Comma in " . . . in the areas of immigration law, personal injury, and criminal defense" but no Oxford Comma in " . . . copyright infringement and valuation of trademarks."
- Fair Use Doctrine should have initial capitalization.
- The employment date ranges are separated with dashes that have inconsistent spacing.

10. Provide references only in limited circumstances. You want to devote as much space on your resumé as possible to fully describing your qualifications. Thus, you should only provide references upon request. There are two exceptions to this rule: if you have recognizable, impressive references (CEO of Nike, US Attorney General, etc.) or have limited relevant experience and need to occupy space, then you should list the name, position, organization and contact information of your professional references.

YOUR COVER LETTER

Your resumé describes your prior relevant experiences and accomplishments. It serves as a snapshot of what you have done so far; an overview of your "story." But your resumé is limited insofar as it is a backward-looking and purely objective document. It neither expresses your future intentions nor the reason why you applied for the internship. This information needs to be conveyed to the organization.

That is why your cover letter is such an important component to your application. Your cover letter should breathe life into your resumé. Focusing on what is most relevant, cover letters seamlessly weave together your past experiences and career aspirations by enlightening the reader as to how and why your background has led you to applying for the internship position at their organization. And it should do so in an engaging, eloquent and endearing way.

The Content of Your Cover Letter

Your cover letter should be one page consisting of four paragraphs — an opening paragraph, two body paragraphs and closing paragraph. The general content of these four paragraphs should be as follows:

First Paragraph: The Opener. This paragraph should provide information that will answer the reader's initial questions, such as your school, year, and what you are applying for (position, timeframe, department, location, full/part time, etc.). If appropriate, your opening paragraph can include information designed to create an initial connection with the reader, such as alumni connection or a referral. Don't become married to the same opening paragraph for every cover letter. The length and content of your opening paragraph should vary depending on the circumstances. Consider the following examples:

Applying for one of three positions posted online:

Dear Mr. Levine:

I am currently a third-year law student applying in response to the online posting for the part-time law clerk in the trust & estates practice department at Kerner & Zagoria LLP.

Referred by a colleague of the hiring attorney:

Dear Ms. Haskell:

At the suggestion of John Moore, I write to submit my application for the full-time summer internship position at the Hudson County District Attorney's Office.

Alumni connection with the hiring attorney:

Dear Ms. Campoli:

I am currently a third-year student at PACE Law School seeking the part-time internship position in the in-house legal department at Eastern Energy, Inc.

Writing to create an internship at small law firm:

Dear Attorney Resnick:

I am a third-year law student at Golden Gate University School of Law writing to inquire whether your firm would be interested in hiring a part-time law clerk to provide assistance with the patent infringement lawsuit recently filed against your client, Vermark Technologies, Inc.

Second Paragraph: Your Story. This paragraph should articulate the part(s) of your "story" that is/are relevant to the position sought. It is your opportunity to explain who you are in a way that makes you an attractive candidate. Because each application demands a specifically-tailored cover letter, it is difficult to instruct on exactly what to write. However, to provide some guidance on potential angles to play and the appropriate tone, structure and word choice, consider the following examples:

Multiple relevant work experiences for an entertainment law internship:

> *For the past five years, I have focused on gaining substantive work experience in entertainment law. Prior to law school, I was a talent agent at United Talent Agency. During law school, I worked as a law clerk at two entertainment law firms and interned in the legal department at AMC Networks. My overall career goal is to work as an entertainment attorney upon graduation and all of these experiences have confirmed my passion for this practice area while enabling me to build and sharpen my relevant skill set.*

This applicant has a string of relevant experiences that he/she listed in support of his/her contention that their goal is to work in that practice area. This is compelling.

A single relevant work experience for a commercial litigation internship at a law firm:

> *This past summer, I worked as a legal intern at the Carson County Public Defender's Office. As reflected on my resumé, I gained extensive practical experience during this internship through my contributions in multiple phases of the litigation process. I was constantly providing results of my legal research and factual investigations to assist the trial attorneys formulate and modify their strategy. My supervisors often used my work product and remarked on my strong research, writing and analytical skills and ability to see the "big picture." I truly enjoyed this experience and it confirmed that a career in litigation is the best fit for me.*

This applicant had only one prior work experience that was relevant to the position sought. Thus, they spent the entire paragraph expounding on that experience with great detail in order to bring it to life for the reader.

The less relevant general or specific experience you have, the trickier it becomes to write this second paragraph. Consider the following scenario: you are applying for an internship at a small real estate firm in Boston. You have no real estate work experience. But you have worked at a small general practice law firm in Boston and received high grades in a real estate-related class.

> *For the past year, I have been working as a part-time law clerk at Kessler & Associates, a general practice law firm in Boston. This experience has and continues to expose me to the pressures and operations of a small firm and teach me how I can best bring value to the team through being dynamic and efficient. I am personable, attentive and responsive to clients, resourceful in my problem-solving and generally willing to do all of the little things to get the job done. I understand that small firms must be flexible, efficient and open to new challenges in order to thrive and this overall approach aligns with my*

"yes attitude" towards assignments. The combination of my experience at Kessler and my recent A+ in Transactional Real Estate class makes me confident that I would do well at a small real estate law firm.

This applicant leveraged all that he/she had — small firm experience and relevant academic success. There is always an angle to play if you are creative and write well.

Third Paragraph: Your Value Proposition. Articulating how you can/will add value to an organization is a skill that will prove extremely useful throughout your career, especially when applying for internships. In its simplest terms, your value proposition is a statement that tells a prospective employer why they should hire you instead of someone else. To construct your unique value proposition, ask the following questions:

About the organization:

- *What does the organization need?*
- *Does the position require some special skill or type of experience?*
- *Is there something special about the organization?*
- *Does the organization have unique pressures?*
- *Has it experienced a recent change?*
- *How does it hold itself out to the public?*

Answering these questions may require referring back to the job position/description or conducting some research, either through an II or online. Think about the organization's needs, interests, pressures, challenges, people, competitors, history, strengths, capabilities, or any other characteristics or circumstances that make the organization or its situation unique.

Then, turn your focus inward and consider what makes you uniquely qualified to fit the position.

About you:

- *What can I do that nobody else can?*
- *What makes me distinctive or unique?*
- *What are my strengths?*
- *Why would they want to hire me over another candidate?*
- *How do I perform better than my peers?*
- *What can I offer that would go above and beyond?*
- *What have my prior employers said about me?*

Use the answers to these questions to uncover your unique value proposition that connects your story with the organization's needs, establishes an emotional connection to the reader and/or explains what differentiates you from the other candidates. There are innumerable ways to accomplish this, just a few of which are demonstrated through the examples below:

They should hire you because you are the perfect fit for the position:

> *As demonstrated above and in my enclosed resumé, I am a highly-qualified candidate for the law clerk position in Kerner & Zagoria LLP's trust & estates department. My academic successes prove that I have a strong aptitude for the applicable legal concepts and my prior work experience will enable me to hit the ground running in this role. Compared to my peers, Kerner will need to devote less time training me and will, therefore, instantly derive a greater value from my work product. In sum, I am confident that I could increase the firm's productivity on day one.*

They should hire you because of your track record:

> *As my resumé reflects, I have a proven track record of academic and professional success. If given the opportunity, I would continue to strive for success by enthusiastically providing assistance to the HCDA Office's attorneys and support staff in their handling of the large number of active litigations for which they are responsible. I will rely upon my strong work ethic, attention to detail and aptitude for learning complex concepts to carry out all that is asked of me. In addition, my flexibility, level-headed personality and ability to perform under pressure will enable me to work harmoniously with your team of professionals.*

They should hire you because you intend to fulfill a particular need:

> *I am interested in an internship at Eastern Energy for the opportunity to assist in revamping EE's employment policies, practices and operations. It is my understanding that EE has recently merged with a competitor and is currently in the process of assimilating the two companies' workforces. As my resumé reflects, I have practical experience researching legal issues and drafting agreements and policies related to the various employment-related situations that will likely arise for EE during this transition period. If given the opportunity, I would apply my practical skills to perform whatever tasks necessary to help make the merger as smooth, efficient and pleasant as possible for EE's management and staff.*

They should hire you because you have a special passion:

> *My first volunteer experience was at a soup kitchen during my sophomore year of high school. This act introduced me to the profound personal satisfaction of selflessly giving back to the community and benefitting the lives of disadvantaged members of our society. As my resumé reflects, I have since continued devoting my efforts to standing up for those in our indigent communities who cannot stand up for themselves and I cannot imagine pursuing a career in any other field. If hired as an intern, my genuine passion for the mission of the Carson County's Public Defenders Office would shine through in my work ethic, attention to detail and unwavering determination to achieve results for our clients.*

If you are struggling to articulate your value proposition, the last option for paragraph three should be resorting to flattery. In an eloquent way and clearly demonstrating that you have done your research, tell the reader specifically why you support and/or are impressed by the organization's mission, longevity, service, uniqueness, people, or recent accomplishments:

I am excited for the opportunity to clerk at Sperver Ketchum & Protter LLP because of its proven track record of success and positive influence in the Richmond community. I trust that a law firm with over 60 years of service must possess strong leadership, talented attorneys, high ethical standards and the ability to adapt as an organization to changing environments. At this point in my legal career, I could greatly benefit from working alongside and learning from the management team, attorneys and support staff who make SKP so successful. Moreover, I admire SKP's support of the various charities in the Richmond area and would be proud to join a group of professionals who, despite their busy schedules and bottom lines, selflessly dedicate time and financial support to organizations that raise the collective spirit of our community. In my opinion, SKP sets a good example for other businesses in Richmond.

Paragraph 4: Next Steps. Your cover letter should conclude with a succinct statement thanking the reader and suggesting possible next steps. Don't tell the reader what to do. Simply lay out whatever might be a reasonable way to proceed under the circumstances. Here are some examples of closing paragraphs:

Thank you in advance for your consideration. If you would like any further materials in connection with my application, please do not hesitate to contact me. I look forward to hearing back from you.

Sincerely,

Christopher P. Riley

I appreciate your time in reviewing the enclosed resumé, writing sample and transcript. Please let me know if you are interested in meeting in person or over the telephone to discuss my candidacy. I will make myself available at your convenience.

Very truly yours,

Alexandra L. Roccio

I am greatly appreciative of your considering my application for the internship position at Eastern Energy, Inc. Please let me know if I can provide any further information in support of my candidacy. Otherwise, I look forward to hearing back from you.

Best regards,

Robert K. Klipper

I will be traveling from Denver to visit the Miami area from January 18 to 28. If convenient for you, I would greatly appreciate the opportunity to meet with you in person to discuss my qualifications further. Either way, thank you for your consideration and I look forward to hearing back from you in the near future.

Yours truly,

Patricia M. Patterson

Ten Cover Letter Drafting Tips

1. Write Eloquently. Along with the requisite qualifications, organizations are always interested in hiring talented writers. Thus, even if you lack the preferred credentials, you may nonetheless impress the reader through writing a cover letter that conveys an original message in a clear, persuasive and endearing way. And in situations where you are competing with equally-qualified candidates, an engaging and extraordinarily well-written cover letter can set you apart.

2. Customize. Before you start writing, sit back and think. Think about what would be the most persuasive and appealing way to write your cover letter. What story do you want to tell? What value proposition do you want to convey? When you are comfortable with your chosen angle, research the organization to add depth and tailor your letter to speak directly to its audience. Reference specific names, events, traits or other characteristics which are unique to the organization. This will create a positive impression that you have done your homework.

3. Use Catchwords. Like your resumé, your cover letter may first be skimmed. To pass this initial inspection, make sure that your cover letter contains verbiage that grabs the reader's attention and focuses them on your qualifications.

4. Don't brag. There is a fine line between describing your accomplishments and overselling yourself. To avoid the latter, write with an undertone of humility. Your resumé should have already set forth your achievements in an objective manner. Thus, as a general rule, you should only discuss your exploits in the cover letter if they are tied to some benefit for the organization. And, if that is the case, be sure to emphasize the benefit, not how great you are.

5. Get names right. Review the cover letter for mistakes, then review it again to confirm that all names are spelled correctly. Nothing will get your cover letter discarded quicker than misspelling the name or address of a recipient or organization.

Side Note: If an organization has a long name, it may be preferable to use some acronym or nickname in certain parts. This is acceptable only if you use an already-established moniker. It is equally distasteful to refer to an organization in a way that it has never approved. Check their website, correspondence or other marketing materials to identify how they refer to themselves. If you cannot find an established moniker, play it safe and stick to reciting the full proper name.

6. Avoid repeating information from your resumé. Space is a precious commodity on your resumé and cover letter. Make sure every word counts. Repeating information is a wasted opportunity and may cause the reader to lose interest or conclude that you are repeating materials because you lack qualifications.

7. No mistakes. As with your resumé, the highest possible standards for grammar, spelling and spacing apply to your cover letter. One errant period or a missing letter can be interpreted by the reader that you have a poor attention to detail or are not serious about your application; both of which will likely result in a rejection.

8. More competition, more unique the cover letter. If you suspect that you are less qualified than others who may be applying for the same position, take more risk with your cover letter. Try being overly precise about your value proposition. Buck the conventional angles and be creative. Weave together a unique theme. Use a quotation, testimonial, slogan or mission statement. You want to be memorable; that may be your best shot at getting hired amongst steep competition.

9. Get an editor. A cover letter is an extremely important document and should be treated as such. That means writing it thoughtfully and editing it thoroughly. Once you finish your first draft, have a trusted peer (law student or lawyer) review it and help you perfect the material, word choice and tone.

10. Don't be pushy. You should be *asking* for an interview. Nothing more. And remember that the organization does not owe you anything. Avoid command-like phrases such as "please contact me upon your review of my resumé to schedule an interview" or "you should give me an opportunity to prove that I would be a valuable addition to the firm." Instead, phrase these same messages as a passive, conditional suggestion "If you have questions regarding my candidacy, please feel free to contact me to discuss. I am available at your convenience."

Manage Your Online Profile

Once you apply for a position, you have now put yourself on that organization's radar. Most inquisitive hiring personnel (attorneys or human resource professionals) will google your name upon receipt your application materials. What will they find?

Be sure that your social media profiles are completely private. Think about the story that you have been working so hard to craft for your potential employer. A perfectly-crafted image of a eager, experienced law student can be instantly tarnished when a hiring personnel sees a picture of you drunk at a bar on your Facebook photos, an angry political message on your Twitter page or a Bob Marley poster on your Pinterest wall. Wait until you get hired and become friendly with the attorneys before inviting them into your personal life.

You should treat Linkedin slightly different. This profile should be public, of course. However, the danger here is that your Linkedin profile will portray a story that differs from the one told in your application. For instance, does your resumé/cover letter highlight your passion for and experience in employment law, but your Linkedin profile emphasize that you are a law student seeking opportunities in real estate law? This type of disjointed presentation can undermine your credibility and damage your application efforts.

If you are going to blog, consider using a penname. Writing fanatically about sports or sharing personal experiences or insights can be extremely rewarding and enjoyable activities. However, they can also interfere with your story from the hiring personnel perspective.

> Side Note: Don't underestimate the hiring personnel by trying to obscure your public social media profile by using differing variations of your name. If your resumé says "Anastasia P. Cleary" but your Facebook profile is "Ana Cleary," expect that they will eventually connect the dots that you go by Ana in your personal life. This is especially true of you are ending your emails to the organization as "Ana."

It's not that you are suppressing who you are or shying away from expressing yourself. Those things are important. What you are doing is affirmatively crafting your professional image by controlling the information available to potential employers. In your application materials, during emails to schedule an interview and during the interview, you are shaping the organization's perception of you. Just be sure that whatever your online personality is, it reinforces that perception. If not, make it private.

Chapter 5

THE INTERVIEW

If you are successful in receiving an offer for an interview, you've now put yourself in an excellent position to get hired. But it is still far from guaranteed. In fact, depending on a number of factors including the organization's needs and level of competition, your chances of getting hired may still be low. Regardless, approach the interview as your final and most powerful opportunity to convince the organization that you are the best fit for the position. It must be your peak performance of the application process.

The Organization's Objective of the Interview

To formulate your strategy for preparing and performing during your interview, it is best to first understand the organization's objective for the interview. But this might not be readily apparent and you must be cautious in assuming why you were offered the interview.

All that is safe for you to deduce from the offer is that the organization views your qualifications as sufficient. Other than that, there are many reasons why they might want to meet with you. The following are a few of the different circumstances and organizational objectives that might be at play for your interview:

- There was steep competition for the position and the interview is needed to choose between multiple, highly-qualified candidates.
- You are the only qualified candidate and they simply want to put a face to the name before extending an offer.
- There is something intriguing, confusing or unique about your resumé they want to discuss and understand better.
- There are inconsistencies or gaps in your resumé/cover letter they want to clear up.
- You were recommended by a valuable contact of the organization, might not have the ideal qualifications but were nonetheless offered an interview as a courtesy to that person.
- The organization is interested in hiring you but wants to ensure that your long-term goals are aligned with theirs.

Your preparation, strategy and performance in this phase of the application process should vary depending on whether you fall under one or more of these scenarios. Regardless, the mystery behind the interview offer makes it a situation-specific endeavor which you enter somewhat blindly.

That being said, there are two common organizational objectives for offering an interview: First, most organizations want to find out if they can connect with you personally and enjoy your company. Second, they want to assess how well they can communicate with you, especially about substantive, legal topics.

Regardless of the twists and turns your interview process may take, be sure to coordinate, prepare for and perform during your interview in a way that accomplishes these two objectives. Doing so will put in you in the best position to get hired.

Coordinating the Interview

Organizations employ different procedures for scheduling interviews. Sometimes, the interviewing/hiring attorney will call or email you directly to propose the date and time. Other times, an administrator will reach out to you. Either way, you should view these correspondences as the first stage of the interview process and ensure you make the right impression. A few rules of thumb regarding these initial communications to schedule the interview:

- **Be concise and clear.** This is a limited purpose communication — set a date, time and location. Make sure you convey no more than the information asked and obtain all the information you need to show up on time to the correct place. It's a huge turnoff for an organization if they are unable to communicate with you efficiently to accomplish a simple objective. Before sending the email, critique every sentence and question whether it *needs* to be in the email. If not, take it out.
- **Be appreciative and professional.** Address the recipient by their last name unless instructed otherwise. Write eloquently. Use formal greetings and closings. Answer the question(s) asked. Be sure to be enthusiastic and appreciative without using exclamation points. Don't send an email that ends with "Sent using my iPhone."
- **Be responsive.** After you apply, be sure to check your email at least once a day to see if there has been a response to your application. Long delays in responding may create the impression that you don't care or are not diligent, neither of which is positive.
- **Find out who will conduct the interview.** There is nothing wrong with asking this question. If the organization hasn't figured it out yet or doesn't want to tell you, then they will decline to specify the interviewer(s). However, knowing this ahead of time will give you an edge when it's time to prepare, as described below.
- **Be available.** Unless absolutely necessary, make yourself available at the date/time/location proposed to you.
- **Opt for in-person interview.** If given the choice, always elect to visit the office and meet in person with the interviewer(s), regardless of the travel costs to you. Do not ask to be reimbursed for travel costs.
- **Don't botch the phone call.** Some interviewers prefer coordinating over the telephone, because it is efficient and gives them an extra opportunity to feel you out. This is a platform for you to perform well. Use it. Be prepared for

substantive questions. Practice beforehand what you would say if you have to leave a voicemail. Don't ramble.

Prepare for the Interview

Your interview is game time. From the organization's perspective, all you have done so far is tell them who you are, what you have done, what you are able to do and what you intend to do for them. That is what got you in the door so far. But talk is cheap.

The interview is your first opportunity to show the organization that you are who you say you are. It is time to perform up to the standards that you have set for yourself. And, like any important performance, you must prepare beforehand. Here are a few preparation pointers:

- **Research the interviewer.** If you know who will be interviewing you, learn as much as you can about them beforehand. Their school, prior employers, practice area, achievements, interests, colleagues, etc. all indicate what they know, who they know and what is important to them. Going into the interview armed with this information will help you illuminate your shared commonalities and avoid expressing conflicting perspectives or values. In sum, the more you know about your interviewer(s), the better chance of impressing them.
- **Research the organization.** Look over the company's website for news events. Did they recently undergo any business, personnel, or industry-wide changes? These are interview topics that can help build rapport and show you are interested in and familiar with what is happening with the company. Use them to formulate questions to the interviewer.
- **Anticipate questions.** The interviewer's questions will act as the outline for the interview. The questions will dictate the topics, length and tone of the interview. If they are easy or personal, the interview may feel like an informal conversation between friends. On the other hand, if the interviewer's questions are difficult or technical, it may feel like an interrogation or test. You want to be as prepared as possible but, as explained above, your blind spots with respect to the circumstances of and organizational objective for the interview make it impossible to predict and prepare for all of the questions that will be asked. That being said, here are some guidelines for anticipating what questions might be asked:
  1. **Be prepared to answer questions related to the position.** *What did the organization emphasize in the job posting? Did they devote effort to detailing any requisite skills? Work experiences? Coursework? Did they write out any particular practice area, organizational objective or project?* Be prepared to answer technical questions about any of the topics that the organization may have identified as important. If there was no posting, be generally prepared to answer technical questions related to your anticipated role at the organization.
  2. **Be prepared to discuss your resumé and cover letter.** *What experiences have you highlighted as important? Skills? Accomplishments? Hobbies? What story have you told in your cover letter?* You should be able answer

the "who, what, where, when, why and how" with respect to anything that you included in your application materials — it is all fair game. This includes answering why you made certain decisions, your values, interests, career goals, why you went to law school, strengths/weaknesses. For technical questions, you must be able to give specific examples.

3. **Be prepared to defend your background.** *Do you have any unexplained gaps in time? Do you have any experiences that are inconsistent with your story? Do you have anything that is missing from your resumé (like GPA/rank)?* Your ability to gracefully navigate these unflattering topics will be crucial. Don't pretend like they don't exist. Recognize your weak points and be prepared to discuss them (see Tip 8 below).

4. **Know your audience.** If the interviewer asks questions about your future intentions or career aspirations, be sure to consider what would appeal to them before answering.

- **Have your own questions.** Questions can be a powerful tool for you during an interview. Not only do questions allow you to obtain important information, but they also are a way to make implied statements that create a positive impression or establish a personal connection. When the time comes, you will likely have an opportunity to ask questions during the interview. Be prepared with a handful of thoughtfully-constructed and carefully-worded questions to accomplish the following six objectives:

1. To gather information about the position to help you decide between potential opportunities, you may want to ask questions like:
   - *What is a typical assignment that I might receive?*
   - *Are there any particular projects that you anticipate involving me in?*
   - *Who will be my supervisors?*

2. To make the implied statement that you have researched and are familiar with the organization, you may want to ask questions like:
   - *Has the real estate group experienced an increase in client demand for compliance advice after the passing of the recent state legislation?*
   - *Would I have the opportunity to contribute to your office's current SEC investigation of the high-profile private equity fund, VAC Capital?*
   - *Has the company's new expansion into Minnesota been a success so far? And if so, would I have an opportunity to work in that office at all?*

3. To make the implied statement that you have experience handling the relevant types challenges or tasks, you may want to ask questions like:
   - *Does the firm use PACER for reviewing the docket for bankruptcy cases online?*

- *What kind of document review software does the company use?*
- *Does the litigation department use the Bluebook standard or ALWD Citation Manual for citations in its briefs?*

4. To make the implied statement that you care about your professional development, you may want to ask questions like:
   - *Is there a formal process for receiving feedback about my work performance?*
   - *Will I have the opportunity to request certain types of work assignments so I can expand my skill set and/or try new things? If so, is there a formal process for this?*
   - *Is there a formal or informal mentorship arrangement at the company?*
5. To establish a connection with the interviewer(s), you may want to ask questions like:
   - *What do you like most about this organization? Dislike?*
   - *What do you like most about your work day? Dislike?*
   - *How did your path lead you to working at this organization?*
6. To make the implied statement that you intend to perform well at their organization if hired, you may want to ask questions like:
   - *What would be the most effective way of preparing for an internship here?*
   - *What are you most looking for in an intern?*
   - *Does the organization ever hire interns as attorneys? If so, how often?*

- **Anticipate logistical issues.** Make sure you arrive 15 minutes early for the interview. This requires understanding and anticipating how you will travel to the location, how long it will take and any potential issues that may arise to cause delays, such as traffic, closures or detours. Regardless of the reason, it will not reflect positively on you if you are late for an interview.
- **Bring adequate materials.** Make sure you have multiple (at least 6) copies of all materials that you submitted in your application as well as those that may be asked of you during an interview, namely, your cover letter, resumé, writing sample, references and transcript. Expect the unexpected when it comes to being asked for a particular document. It's better to have it and not need it, then to need it and not have it. Also bring a pen and notepad.
- **Practice, practice and practice.** Whether to a mirror in your bathroom, softly to yourself during your commute or aloud to a trusted peer, you must practice saying aloud the answers to anticipated questions. Pay attention to what you are saying and how you are saying it. Be self-critical. If it doesn't sound right to you, it probably won't sound right to the interviewer(s). Continue to practice until you've built clear, concise and substantively rich statements. Tweak word choice and tone so you sound endearing, genuine and

professional. Practice will help perfect your content and delivery.

10 Tips for Strong Performance during the Interview

As with any sport, strong performance during your interview will depend on a variety of factors that are impossible to predict. After adequately preparing for the interview, the best advice to follow is just to be yourself. You are there because you deserve to be there. Now it's time to let your personality, intelligence and knowledge shine through. For some additional guidance, here are a few performance tips:

1. Present well — Men should be shaved or well-groomed facial hair. Women should not overdo their makeup. Clothes should be clean, plain and fit properly. Do not wear anything flashy or revealing. Your physical appearance should not be memorable in any meaningful way.

2. Manage Stress — Pay attention to your anxiety level. If you are too worked up, practice some stress-relieving exercises. Nothing will block your intellect more than anxiety. You want to be loose going into the interview, feeling confident and on-point.

3. Be polite to administrative staff — Receptionists, secretaries, paralegals, clerks or other support staff may appear unimportant, but they are not. Treat each of them as if they are the one making your hiring decision. Depending on their tenure, the structure of the organization or the difficulty of the hiring attorney to decide between candidates, support staff may be asked for their impression of you.

4. Take water — Water is a basic need. You will not be putting them out by asking for it. It is certainly no imposition if they already offered. Taking a sip of water during an interview will quench your thirst, clear your throat, help your voice to travel further and can also be a good way to channel any nervous energy you may have.

5. Remember the basics — Make sure you shake hands with your interviewer(s), exchange pleasantries, thank them for their time, make eye contact, hold doors and engage in whatever small talk the interviewer(s) may initiate. Feel free to laugh when things are funny (or when you notice that the interviewer is *trying* to be funny). Don't stop acting like a normal human being just because it is an interview.

6. Don't ramble — The interview should flow like any other conversation, each person speaking and listening in equal parts. If anything, it is better that the interviewer(s) speak more than you. Don't let your nerves get the best of you and cause you to ramble. Pay close attention to what is asked, breath, think, formulate the answer in your head and respond with no more than what is necessary to answer the question. It is better to have a short answer that neglects a minor point than to bury the answer within a five-minute soliloquy filled with gratuitous information. Concisely answering a direct question is a necessity for all attorneys. You must be able to do it.

7. Talk turkey — If you are hired as an intern, you will likely discuss legal issues, present research, brainstorm about strategy, report facts and generally engage in discourse that is complicated and technical. Moreover, you will do so in a busy work environment where time is limited and efficient communication is critical. Interviewers ask technical questions to get a glimpse into how well you can communicate these issues in that environment. You must be able to explain a legal problem, case, issue, matter or other past experiences like an attorney. This may take extra practice beforehand.

8. Stay positive, even on negative topics — There may be some aspects of your background that reflect negatively on your performance, such as getting fired from a previous position, receiving a low grade or a poor reference. If the topic of conversation ventures into these areas, don't criticize anyone else or blame circumstances. Own the experience and use it as an opportunity to explain how you have learned from mistakes, improved and developed. This will also take practice beforehand.

9. Act professional and humble — Sit up straight at all times. If anything, you should lean forward to indicate with body language that you are listening intently. Avoid using speech fillers such as "like," "um" and "you know." Speak slowly, deliberately and change intonation to keep the interviewer's attention. Keep in mind that, as a law student, attorneys will likely view you as knowing very little. For that reason, you should be careful not to overstate your knowledge or understanding. Try to weave in slight disclaimers such as "I know I'm only scratching the surface on this, but it appears . . . " or "In my limited experience . . . " Being a know-it-all is off-putting.

10. Keep the conversation going — Generally speaking, the longer the interview, the better the chance that you will establish a personal connection with the interviewer. Unless there is a definitive stop time for the interview and there are certain points that you want to cover in a limited period of time, continue discussing each topic to its natural end. If you feel an awkward silence creeping in, that's the time to chime in with "Can I ask a question?" Then ask one of your prepared questions. That will revive the conversation and hopefully introduce more topics and questions.

Last Question of the Interview

After the interview is complete and the conversation is winding down to a close, ask about their process for making the decision:

- *How many more candidates do you anticipate interviewing for this position?*
- *Do you have an idea of when you will be making the hiring decision for this position?*

These are fair questions to ask and will give you a sense of how to proceed forward after the interview with respect to your other applications. They will also help relieve any anxiety you may have while waiting to hear back after the interview.

Follow up

On the day of or after the interview, send a follow up email to the interviewer(s) thanking them for the opportunity to meet with them, confirming that you are still interested and eager to work at their organization, offering to send further materials and any other information that may be relevant. The email is more of a gesture than informational. It is simply to have your name resonating in a positive way while they are deliberating who to hire. It should be short and sweet. Here's an example of a basic follow up email:

Dear Mr. Cantor:

Thank you so much for taking the time to meet with me today. I truly enjoyed speaking with you and our discussions confirmed my desire to work at Kerner Totter LLP as a law clerk.

If you would like to review any additional materials in connection with my application or discuss the details of my candidacy further, please let me know.

Otherwise, I look forward to hearing back from you.

Very truly yours,

Christoper N. Locker

In addition, you might want to consider mailing a handwritten note to the interviewing attorney. Sometimes these types of personalized gestures can make you stand out from your competition.

Responding to an Offer/Declination

If you receive a declination email, letter or telephone call, be sure to politely thank them for their consideration. Don't be sour grapes and either send back something snarky or don't respond at all. Be professional.

A more complicated situation arises if you receive an offer from Employer A while waiting to hear back from Employer B. If this happens, and you feel compelled to wait for Employer B's decision, be upfront with Employer A. Endearingly thank them for their offer and politely ask if you can have some time to decide whether to accept. This is a totally reasonable request. Nobody should fault you for taking your time to think through a very important decision. If Employer A agrees to give you limited period of time to decide, then promptly contact Employer B, tell them of the situation also and politely ask if they could give you an answer sooner than anticipated.

Obviously, if you receive an email or telephone call offering you a position that you want to accept, say or write "Yes." Easy enough!

PART III:

THE THREE GOALS FOR YOUR LEGAL INTERNSHIP

Now that you've been hired, it's time to shift your mind state and focus on how to gain the most value from your internship and perform to the best of your ability.

Looking ahead, your internship is going to place you into unfamiliar work environments and circumstances, surrounded by new coworkers and supervisors, grappling with difficult assignments, deadlines and subject matter and feeling different kinds of pressures and emotions. Overall, this can be an intimidating and somewhat overwhelming experience. You are obviously going to work hard. *But what are you working for?*

Your internship goals will perpetually answer that question. They will act as a compass when you become disoriented and keep you heading in the right direction. Your goals will also be a source of motivation during difficult times. For these and many more reasons, countless research studies have shown a direct correlation between goal-setting and enhanced work performance.

And here's the overarching point: if you have obtained the *right* internship and achieve the *right* goals during that internship, then you will take the largest possible stride down your best-suited career path. Give yourself this opportunity, which starts by setting your **specific** and **overall** internship goals.

Your specific internship goals should be tailored to your career aspirations. For example, a student pursuing intellectual property law may have a specific goal of learning how to file a trademark application or a student pursuing a career in litigation may have a specific goal of contributing to a deposition or trial. Set your specific goals beforehand and keep them in the forefront of your mind during your internship.

You may also consider meeting with a law school professor or career advisor prior to your internship to review your specific goals and assess whether they are realistic, how to go about seeking out opportunities to achieve them, and to create viable alternatives if your specific goals are unattainable for reasons outside of your control. This will help bring clarity to your specific goals, help you to articulate them to your supervising attorney during your internship, and formulate an action plan for achieving them.

> *What are the specific goals for your internship? Do you want to gain experience in a particular practice area? Broaden your knowledge of civil procedure? Assist with a deposition? Work in a particular industry? Participate in the negotiation of a commercial contract?*

Be aware, however, that internships are unpredictable experiences. The organization's needs (not your specific goals) will ultimately dictate the work that you perform during your internship. Put plainly, if nobody needs it, you are not doing it. Therefore, you should mentally prepare for the possibility that you may not achieve your specific goals.

That is why, no matter where you work, you should always complement your specific goals with the following three overall internship goals:

1. **Learn practical legal skills;**
2. **Create working relationships with attorneys; and**
3. **Develop as a professional.**

Remain focused on these three goals and make certain that at least one underpins every task that you carry out. If you do that, you will maximize your work performance and extract the most value from the internship.

Track Your Progress

During your internship, pay attention to whether and how you are achieving your specific and overall goals. This is an effective way to hold yourself accountable and stave off procrastination. Sometimes keeping a log, diary or simply emailing yourself can suffice to keep a record of your progress towards your goals. As you assess your progress periodically, provide honest feedback to yourself and adjust as you go along.

Albert Einstein said: "[t]he measure of intelligence is the ability to change." Be flexible and stay intelligently focused on your goals. If you reach a roadblock, don't give up. Shift gears, change your approach or mindset and continue marching forward.

> *What have been your professional goals so far? Have you achieved them? Have you adjusted your goals? How do you measure your large and small accomplishments? Do you measure them at all?*

Obstacles to Achieving Your Goals

The internship experience can be a rocky road. You should enter it with eyes wide open and cognizant of potential obstacles that can derail you from pursuing your goals. At some point during your internship, you will inevitably face challenges, lose focus, experience fatigue, make mistakes or receive negative feedback. Such circumstances may lead to feelings of discouragement, insecurity or frustration, making you vulnerable to adopting a jaded or pessimistic outlook. In these moments, be resilient and persist towards your goals. Otherwise, you may fall victim to diverging away from your *goals* in favor of your *desires.*

Desires are the antithesis of goals. Yet, few people appreciate the difference between the two. Ray Dalio, the owner of Bridgewater Capital who is famous for his business success and unique management style, in his volume "Principles," articulates the relationship between a goal and a desire:

> *Goals are the things that you really want to achieve, while desires are the things you want that can prevent you from reaching your goals. . . . For example, a goal might be physical fitness, while a desire is the urge to eat good-tasting, unhealthy food . . . that could undermine you obtaining your fitness goals. So, in terms of the consequences they produce, goals are good and desires are bad.*

As you progress through your internship, be wary of your desires and how they can impede the achievement of your goals. Some desires that may arise during a legal internship are:

- wanting to finish an assignment quickly to move onto something else;
- wanting to avoid types of assignments that you find boring or overwhelming;
- wanting to be considered the smartest or the best;
- wanting recognition or advancement; or
- wanting to avoid people that you do not like.

These are not noble pursuits; they are hollow desires that can distract or prevent you from achieving your goals. When performing your work, ask yourself whether you are pursuing a goal, or a desire. If it is simply a desire, *without judging yourself,* redirect your energy towards your goals.

What motivates you to work hard and succeed? Do you tend to focus on short-term desires or long term goals? Have you ever been distracted by a desire that prevented your achievement of a goal?

Chapter 6

LEARN PRACTICAL LEGAL SKILLS

"For the things we have to learn before we can do them, we learn by doing them." Aristotle

One of the best ways to stand out amongst your peers is through demonstrated practical ability. A law school graduate will be highly marketable if they can "hit the ground running" and add immediate value to an organization with minimal training. You can fit this description by acquiring as many practical legal skills as possible during school.

By far, participating in a legal internship is the most efficient way to gain these skills. However, the extent to which you acquire skills during an internship can vary dramatically. For instance, if your work atmosphere is hectic, you may end up bouncing from one assignment to another, thoughtlessly scrambling to get your work done. This will result in many missed learning opportunities. Be sure to meet your workplace demands, but also remain focused on investing in your own learning at the same time.

To do this, it is imperative that you understand the science of experiential learning — the process of acquiring new skills through practical experiences. If you can incorporate this science into your workday, your performance will improve faster than your peers, your skill set will expand further, you will likely have an easier time getting a job and your transition from academia to practice will be much smoother. Experiential learning opportunities will be all around you during your internship. Take advantage.

This chapter will walk through the science of experiential learning and demonstrate how you can apply its principles during your internship in order to maximize your acquisition of practical legal skills.

Types of Practical Legal Skills

By definition, a practical skill is any skill that is useful. Thus, your challenge will be to learn the practical skills that attorneys use. Because lawyers are essentially problem-solvers, their practical legal skills are far too varied to list exhaustively. However, the following is a sample of some of the skills you should be seeking to learn during your internship:

- Analytical Skills — knowledge of substantive law and legal procedure, identifying issues, eliminating unrealistic outcomes, evaluating exposure, hedging and minimizing risk, assimilating information from multiple sources, designing strategies for resolution, motivating and coordinating action from multiple parties, interpreting behavior or sets of facts.

- Research and Writing Skills — conducting legal research, using legal research software, writing memoranda, letters, emails, articles, summaries of meetings or events, drafting contracts and other documents used in practice, editing/revising documents and citing to legal authority.
- Communication Skills — oral communication, public speaking, client counseling, keen listening skills and issue-spotting, status reporting, developing themes and strategically-arranging facts, persuasive writing, negotiating, investigating, relationship-building, client pitches and marketing.

What are you able to do right now? What practical legal skills do you possess? Do you stand out because of your practical skills? If not, how do you stand out among your peers? Does your resumé completely and accurately reflect what you could accomplish on day one of an attorney job?

PRACTICAL LEGAL SKILLS ARE TRANSFERRED THROUGH EXPERIENCE

All practical legal skills are rooted in "tacit knowledge" — the type of knowledge that is difficult to transfer by writing down or verbalizing it. That is why you must *experience* the practice of law in order to acquire the skills. This is how attorneys have acquired them.

Through their experiences, attorneys develop a heightened sensitivity to important information in a given situation and rely on their tacit knowledge to identify what action should be taken in response to that information. In a sense, attorneys are hired to "see around corners" or two steps ahead for their clients.

> *Example: The multiple phases of litigation illustrate this concept well. Litigations begin with the pleadings (complaint, notice, summons, answer, counterclaims, etc.). This is the phase where the parties give notice of their claims and carve out the scope of the lawsuit. The decisions made at this step will determine the forum, who is involved, what allegedly happened and the relief sought. The next step in litigation is discovery (interrogatories, document demands, depositions, etc.). This is when the parties exchange information. An attorney must look back to the pleadings to determine what information is within the scope of the lawsuit and think ahead to identify what information is needed to prove their claims. At trial/summary judgment phase, dispositive decisions on the lawsuit are made by the court or jury. How well a litigant proves their claims using the information acquired in discovery will ultimately determine whether the court/jury issues a decision in their favor. The more practical experience an attorney obtains at each phase of litigation, the more tacit knowledge they acquire and the sharper their litigation strategy.*

Your goal should be to gain tacit knowledge in order to build your practical skill set. To do this, attorneys need to transfer their tacit knowledge to you, and the most effective way to do this is through extensive personal contact, regular interaction and trust. In other words, tacit knowledge is transferred through *practice.*

This is why a legal internship is perhaps one of the only ways to truly acquire practical legal skills during law school. You cannot absorb these skills from a book or during a lecture; they *must* be transferred from attorneys to you during an internship.

The Experiential Learning Cycle

Here is how experiential learning works: Each time you are given an assignment during your internship, you begin a cycle of learning. This "Learning Cycle," as coined by famous professor of organizational behavior and psychology David Kolb, is broken down into four stages, depicted in the graphic below:

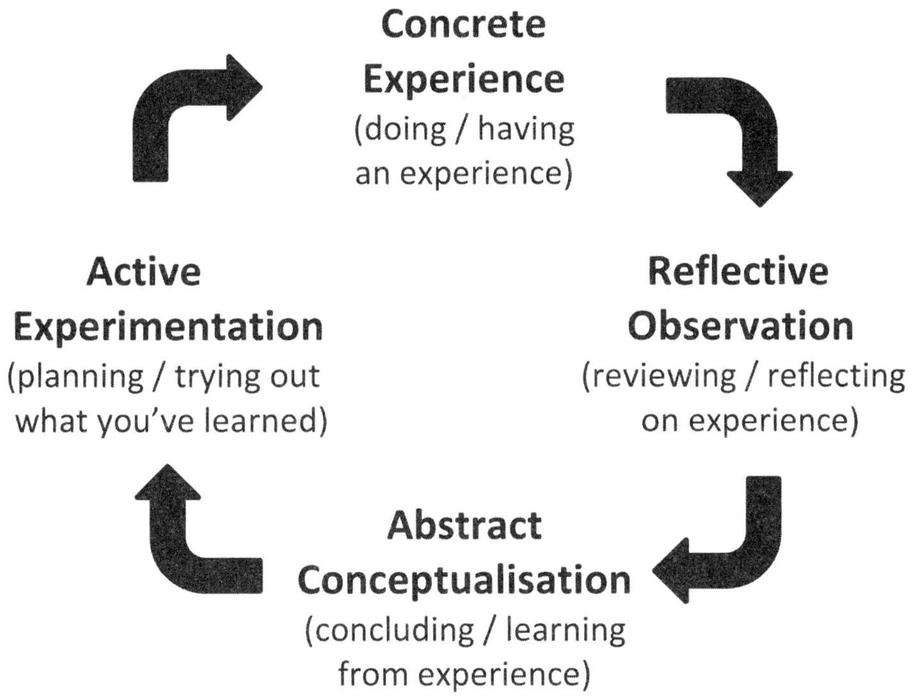

- Stage One is a ***concrete experience***, where you actually perform the assignment.
- Stage Two is ***reflective observation***, where you reflect back on the assignment to make sense of it and uncover any inconsistencies between the experience and what you previously understood.
- Stage Three is ***abstract conceptualism***, where you conduct your own independent research and exploration on the subject matter to cultivate new ideas about what you learned.

- Stage Four is ***active experimentation***, where you perform the assignment (or similar assignment) again and apply your newly-acquired knowledge.

To bring these concepts to life, let's venture a bit deeper into the Learning Cycle and explore each stage within the context of your legal internship. Appreciating the importance of and consciously participating in each stage will ensure that you learn as much as possible from each assignment.

Stage 1: Concrete Experience (Performing the Assignment)

Your concrete experiences during your internship are the moments where you are performing a task for the first time — your assignments. While there are countless types of assignments you may receive as an intern, the following is a sample of tasks that you could expect to do:

- Conduct legal research and write memoranda with conclusions (conclusions are sometimes written via email or reported verbally).
- Review documents/contracts to spot issues, aggregate information, summarize facts, make grammatical edits or cite check legal authorities.
- Compile and/or organize documents in connection with a litigation or transaction;
- Attend and/or provide assistance to an attorney during an event where they are performing legal services, such as a meeting, court appearance, deposition, mediation, conference call, etc.
- Write first drafts of letters, court filings, contracts, and other work product.
- Write marketing articles, create multi-state legal surveys, perform non-legal research on trends, events, or people or other ancillary assignments that attorneys *want* to do but don't have the time.

These are the types of projects that attorneys typically feel comfortable assigning to an intern. Ideally, your assignment will be given to you by an attorney who will explain the background facts and applicable law, provide instructions/tips on how to complete the assignment, answer questions as you perform the assignment, review and give feedback on your work product, and finalize the assignment in your presence. However, in reality, the typical law office is busy and attorneys are trained in practicing law, not teaching it. The following scenario is far more likely to resemble your concrete experience during an internship:

> *Case Study Assignment: An attorney assigns you to write a letter to the Securities and Exchange Commission to request that the client, a venture capital fund, be exempt from registering with the SEC. The assigning attorney briefly explains the client's background and asks you to submit the letter by the close of business the following day. You then research the venture capital exemption, draft the letter and deliver it to the attorney three hours before the deadline. You receive no feedback nor do you see the final version of the letter.*

This assignment touched on a few, but not all of the steps in the ideal concrete experience. You were assigned "real" work to do, given some background information on the client and situation, had time to do your own background research and were able to turn the assignment in early. But the lack of feedback kept you somewhat in the dark about how well you performed the assignment.

To an intern that does not understand the power of experiential learning, this would be the end of the assignment. But there is much more to be learned from this concrete experience as you continue on the Learning Cycle.

Stage 2: Reflective Observation (Questioning Your Work)

The next stage, reflective observation, is the time to engrave the assignment in your mind and learn from it. This is done by evaluating how you achieved your intended goals and which aspects of your performance require further attention.

Reflection can take place in many ways. Due to the time constraints and likely lack of any "facilitators," the most realistic method of reflection during an internship will be to engage in an internal discourse. The following table shows the topics for your internal discourse in the context of the SEC letter case study assignment:

Stage	**General Question**	**Follow Up Questions**	**SEC Letter Example**
Description	***What happened?*** Don't make judgments. Just describe it to yourself.	*What did I do? What role did I play? What was the result?*	I created a first draft of a letter for the attorney to work off of. My role was to get him started. I have not learned the final result.
Analysis	***What is my analysis of the experience?*** Incorporate ideas from outside the assignment to help make sense of the experience.	*What did I do well? What went wrong? What did others do well/ poorly?*	My writing was clear and concise. But I had minimal knowledge of important background facts. If the assigning attorney would have told me those facts, I could have created better work product.

Stage	General Question	Follow Up Questions	SEC Letter Example
Conclusion	***What can be deduced?*** Use the results of the analysis to reach conclusion.	*What could have been done better? What could have been the better outcome?*	There could have been more information exchanged in the initial meeting with assigning attorney. The letter could have included more detail on the client, which would have made it more persuasive.
Action Plan	***What is the plan for the future?*** Identify steps you would do differently in the future.	*If this assignment arises again, what will I do differently? What steps would I take?*	I will ask more questions of the assigning attorney related to the background facts and client. If the initial meeting has to be brief, I will set up a time with the assigning attorney to ask follow up questions or send them a follow-up email.

Find time to ask these questions, answer them honestly and make note of the truths uncovered. If you have the time and energy, keep a log or diary. The more quality time you spend reflecting on your experiences, the deeper you will understand your abilities, strengths, weaknesses, preferences and whether you enjoy the work.

But there is still more to be gained from this experience. Continue on to the next stage of the Learning Cycle.

Stage 3: Abstract Conceptualism (Researching the Big Picture)

"Abstract conceptualism" is the stage of the Learning Cycle where you engage in an independent inquiry to learn how your assignment fits into the big picture. It builds on the concrete experience and reflection stages by introducing the theories underlying what you have done and why you have done it.

Examples of ways that you should engage in abstract conceptualism during your internship include:

- Conducting independent research by reviewing/analyzing primary and secondary sources such as treatises, legislative history, law review articles or case law.
- Reading relevant current events, articles, blogs or books that involve the relevant subject matter of your assignment.
- Asking substantive questions to an experienced professional with relevant experience.

Your independent research will bring new context, clarity and depth to your understanding of the assignment. This, in turn, increases the proficiency of your practical legal skills. Continuing with the same sample SEC letter assignment:

> Case Study Assignment (cont'd): *To engage in abstract conceptualism, you start by reading a treatise giving an overview of the venture capital exemption. Then, you read the legislative history to learn the purpose of the exemption, its history and relation to other exemptions to securities filing requirements. You then read a law review article and consider criticisms and proposed changes to the exemption. If this particular exemption is under recent scrutiny, you could search for news articles/blogs to learn its relevance today. During the course of your research there will likely be conceptual or practice-related questions that arise. You could then reach out to a corporate attorney to ask these questions. This would be the ideal abstract conceptualism.*

After conducting the independent research, you can now see a clear, up-to-date, and 360-degree view of the concrete experience. This, in turn, boosts competence and confidence in this area and positions you for success in future assignments. It is the intersection between practice and theory and brings meaning and relevance to the work.

Stage 4: Active Experimentation (Test Your Skills)

Engaging in "active experimentation" is, on its face, no different than a concrete experience. Except this time around, you are applying your newly-acquired skills. You filled in the "what" during your initial concrete experience. You then filled in the "how" during your reflective observation. You then filled in the "why" when you conducted your independent research in the abstract conceptualism stage. Now, it is time to test all that you have learned. The active experimentation stage is where you test the "what if."

> Case Study Assignment (cont'd): *If asked to write another letter to the SEC regarding a venture capital fund exemption or a similar assignment, relying on what you learned during the Learning Cycle, you could test:*
>
> - *What if I wrote a more stridently worded letter to the SEC?*
> - *What if I addressed the intended purpose behind that the venture capital fund exemption?*

- *What if I sent the letter with the client's letterhead and signature, not the firm's?*
- *What if I included a greater amount of background information on the purpose of the fund?*
- *What if I cited some portions of the legislative history?*
- *What if I called the SEC attorney before sending the letter?*

It may be the same assignment, but at this stage, you know more and can do it better. You have been through it, reflected on it and researched around it. You gained tacit knowledge through witnessing how the initial assignment turned out. Now you're ready to do it again with increased confidence, proficiency, accuracy and perhaps creativity. This is how *good* becomes *great.*

And, here's why it is a "cycle": once you are engaging in active experimentation, consider yourself back at the beginning. Strap in for another go-around becoming increasingly proficient at your work. This is what lawyers do on a daily, weekly, monthly and yearly basis. This is how they continue to deepen their tacit knowledge and master their craft. As an intern, you should seek out every opportunity to engage in the same learning process.

Active Observation (Watch and Learn)

Attorneys can also facilitate the transference of tacit knowledge to interns through "active observation." As opposed to experiential learning (which revolves around *the intern's* experience performing legal work), active observation only requires the intern to be present during *the attorney's* work. It is the easiest way for an attorney to create learning opportunities for an intern.

Generally speaking, opportunities for active observation arise in any situation where an attorney is preparing for or carrying out an aspect of their job, such as:

- Conducting a client meeting;
- Appearing in court for a conference, to argue a motion or conduct a hearing/trial;
- Conducting a deposition, fact-gathering inquiry or investigation;
- Taking a conference call on speaker phone;
- Reading and responding to an email from a client, colleague or adversary;
- Analyzing the law/facts and drafting various types of substantive documents like letters, memoranda, affidavits, complaints, or answers; and/or
- Thinking through a case and crafting discovery demands like interrogatories, document demands, requests to admit, etc.

While they are carrying out these tasks, attorneys must focus on their work and, therefore, this may not be the right time to ask questions. Instead, you should spend time observing what they are doing/not doing and writing down questions that arise. What you observe should be black and white — your questions should be geared towards filling in the color. The standard "who, what, why, where, when and how" typically suffice to paint the full picture.

> Case Study Assignment (cont'd): *The assigning attorney finalizes your draft of the letter, signs it and sends it to the SEC. You get a copy of the letter and compare it to your draft and notice the edits that the attorney made. You notice that the attorney shortened many of your sentences, changed some word choices and added some facts of which you were unaware. Then you craft some questions about the choices that she made and ask her:*
>
> - *"Why did you remove my citations to the applicable statute?" Attorney responds: "There is only one statute applicable to our situation and the SEC knows what it is. I didn't want to waste space on the letter telling them something they already know."*
> - *"Why did you change my comma after the SEC attorney's name to a colon?" Attorney responds: "Typically, we put commas when writing someone with whom we are familiar and have a collegial relationship. Colons are for more formal correspondence, especially to the government."*
> - *Why did you remove my statement offering to assist them in the event they want to investigate further?" Attorney responds: "The SEC tries to resolve these matters without using their limited resources conducting an investigation, especially if the amount of money at issue is relatively low. I want them to presume that we will not be cooperative and, if they elect to investigate, it will be a long and difficult process for them. Depending on their current caseload, this may be the deciding factor in whether to approve our exemption or investigate further."*

You wouldn't have known what changes were made if you didn't thoroughly review the final draft of the letter. And, perhaps more importantly, you wouldn't have known *why* the changes were made if you didn't ask the attorney.

Learning why lawyers choose certain actions over others provides insight into the development of legal strategy — another highly valuable practical skill that can be acquired through active observation.

Everyone Learns Differently

Keep in mind that everyone naturally gravitates toward certain stages of the Learning Cycle or active observation based upon their learning style, which is largely shaped by their background, experience and personality. The most impactful learning experiences, however, will occur when one engages in a manner of experiential learning that does not naturally suit them (i.e., someone who prefers independent research engages in concrete experience). This is yet another reason why understanding "who you are" and how you learn will help you succeed.

> *How do you prefer to learn? Do you find that you most effectively pick up concepts or new skills when you are actively engaged in "doing"? Or do you*

prefer observing and analyzing someone else do the work? Which stage of the learning cycle is most appealing to you?

Final Thoughts on Learning Practical Legal Skills

Practical legal skills help us stand out from our peers and are the tools of an attorney's trade. Opportunities to learn these skills are waiting for you during a legal internship. Some internships will be plush with opportunities while others may not. Some concrete experiences will be fully-guided by attorneys and others will be solo missions. Either way, you *need* to understand what practical legal skills are and the science behind learning them. That way, regardless of your internship environment, you can identify and seize on every possible chance to expand your practical legal skill set and position yourself for success.

Chapter 7

CREATE WORKING RELATIONSHIPS WITH ATTORNEYS

"The most important single ingredient in the formula of success is knowing how to get along with people."
Theodore Roosevelt

As mentioned earlier in the book, positive professional relationships within the legal community are a key ingredient to initial and continued success throughout your career. The most valuable of all professional relationships are "working relationships" with attorneys, which can only be developed by law students during their legal internships. When you graduate, there may be barriers to getting attorney jobs in certain industries or organizations. Working relationships with attorneys may be your best bet for breaking through those barriers.

A working relationship is the relationship cultivated between two professionals who work together to achieve a common objective. A unique bond is shared when we work together, especially if the work is performed under pressure, up against a deadline or to achieve a high-stakes objective. In these moments, our true colors are revealed, and working relationships are created. Some ways these relationships are created and strengthened include:

- Relying on each other to work independently for a common purpose;
- Trusting that the work product created and/or conclusions reached are well-thought out and correct;
- Witnessing each other working under pressure and perhaps becoming agitated or upset;
- Learning about one another's strengths, weaknesses, preferences, sense of humor, and perhaps personal life; and/or
- Sharing in and dealing with success and failure.

If you are fortunate enough to share these experiences with other lawyers during your internship, then you may introduce into your life what I refer to as a "working relationship attorney." Working relationship attorneys can be long-lasting and influential allies in your career.

How many working relationships do you have with attorneys? How did you develop a working relationship with them? What did you work on? What did you learn about them? What did they learn about you? Are you still in touch with these attorneys? If not, why not?

THE IMPORTANCE OF WORKING RELATIONSHIPS WITH ATTORNEYS

Attorneys operate at the center of the robust legal industry. They are walking, talking small businesses regardless of whether they are self-employed, employed by the government, in-house at a company, or at a law firm. The services attorneys provide create jobs for other attorneys, as well as for numerous other types of professionals working in the legal industry.

This prominent position in the legal industry makes attorneys' work experience relevant and valuable, plugs them into channels of important information and bolsters the potency of their opinions and recommendations.

The following sections explain the three most important reasons why it should be your goal to develop relationships, especially working relationships, with attorneys during your internship.

1. Provide Meaningful Career Guidance

Access to credible, reliable guidance is a necessity for any career, especially a legal career, which tends to have considerable lateral mobility. The decisions made during law school will largely shape the direction and trajectory of your career after graduation, and you should not make these decisions without the input of someone who has traveled down the path already.

Through being engaged in the workforce today, attorneys are privy to all sorts of information that is valuable, exclusive and/or only attainable within certain networks, including:

- Current pressures and emerging trends in the marketplace and job market;
- Unwritten rules, structures and customs defining a particular organization's culture;
- How to avoid common mistakes as you pursue your career;
- The identity of/contact information for influential people; and
- Sources of information concerning continuing education or networking opportunities.

Attorneys can reflexively share information off the top of their head, discard misperceptions and clear up misunderstandings that you may have. Their wisdom in this area is real and useful. Just a few examples of how solid career advice can positively influence the pursuit of your chosen career:

- *If you wanted to work as a prosecutor at the district attorney's office, a practicing prosecutor or criminal attorney could tell you which conferences, networking events or associations are most effective for networking in the criminal prosecution community and which ones can be a waste of time.*
- *If you wanted to broaden your knowledge in civil procedure, a practicing litigator could recommend certain continuing education programs or semi-*

nars that they know to be informative and useful.

- *If you wanted an in-house position, a practicing in-house attorney could help evaluate your experience and identify what other types of experience you should get to increase the likelihood of landing an in-house job.*

Moreover, because they have worked with you, your *working relationship attorneys* can provide you with a special kind of career advice. Specifically, based on what they have observed about your strengths and weaknesses, they can provide tailored, constructive feedback on what opportunities or career paths *are most suitable and realistic for you.* This type of guidance is priceless.

> *What questions do you need answered to move forward with your career? From whom do you seek career guidance? Do you speak with practicing attorneys? What are their credentials? What is their professional experience? How qualified are they to provide you with the advice you are seeking? Who do you know that would be qualified?*

2. Share Information About Jobs

It is widely-accepted that the *vast majority* of job vacancies are never advertised. This ocean of job opportunities inconspicuously absent from websites or publications is commonly referred to as the "hidden job market."

While there are few definitive statistics as to the size of this hidden job market, information gleaned from the U.S. Bureau of Labor Statistics suggests that the portion of total job openings filled through word of mouth is somewhere around 70%. There is no reason to believe that the hidden job market within the legal profession is any different.

Attorneys are plugged directly into this hidden legal job market. They are the job creators, decision-makers and facilitators in a constant flow of exclusive job information within the legal community. Before the job posting appears on a job search website, a law school's career services' office, a legal recruiter's inbox or craigslist, *it is an attorney* who first identifies the need to hire a new attorney. And when a position becomes available in the hidden job market, attorneys email and telephone each other to seek referrals. If you are successful in developing relationships with attorneys during your internship — especially working relationships — they will think of you during these interactions.

3. Provide Persuasive Recommendations

Law students make two common mistakes when seeking help from practicing attorneys in their job search. First, they expect or rely on attorneys in their professional network to hire them. This is a highly unlikely outcome. Of course, if an attorney wants and has the opportunity to hire you, then you're all set. However, statistically speaking, it is more likely that it would be an attorney's weak contacts who hire you. Thus, you should count on the attorneys in your network to *write recommendations* on your behalf, not hire you.

This leads to the second most common mistake — students asking an attorney to vouch for their work performance if they have not worked with that attorney. Do not do this. Each time an attorney writes a recommendation, they put their reputation on the line. Because it takes an entire career to build a reputation, attorneys will not risk tarnishing it to help you get a job. And it is unprofessional to ask them to do so. For this reason, a recommendation from a non-working relationship attorney has limited value, as they cannot (and likely will not) speak to your work performance.

This is where the true value of a *working* relationship with an attorney shines through. Nobody has a greater ability than your working relationship attorneys to write a credible and convincing recommendation on your behalf *with specific examples*. The power of a recommendation from a working relationship attorney is aptly-illustrated through the following three emails to a potential hiring attorney:

<u>From an attorney who is family/friend:</u>

> *Hey Greg,*
>
> *My brother Jared just applied for an attorney position at your office. Any help you can give would be much appreciated.*
>
> *Best,*
>
> *Laurent*

There is little else the recommending attorney can write in this situation, if they decide to write at all. Of course, having connections certainly creates opportunities. But it is far more likely that a candidate will be selected based on merit, not who they know — this is particularly true in the legal field. And if the relationship between the friend/family attorney and the hiring attorney is somewhat attenuated, it can be an awkward or worse, tacky, email to write.

<u>From an attorney you met at a networking event:</u>

> *Hey Greg,*
>
> *I write to recommend Jared for an attorney position at your office.*
>
> *I recently met Jared at a networking event. He is a personable and bright guy. We spoke for a while about the law and he seems like he would be a good fit for the position.*
>
> *Best,*
>
> *Laurent*

This email has slightly more substance because the recommending attorney connected with you about serious, legally-related issues and they enjoyed your company. But they cannot represent that they *know* that you are a good candidate for the position. All they know is what you told them. And the hiring attorney recognizes this is hearsay.

From a working-relationship attorney:

Hey Greg,

I write to recommend Jared for an attorney position at your office.

Jared is a former intern at my firm with whom I worked well in excess of 200 hours. I can attest, from personal, first-hand knowledge, that Jared is a hard-working, intelligent and personable person. He picks up concepts quickly, is trustworthy, reliable and easy to work with. Specifically, he did an outstanding job researching and writing a dispositive motion.

Based on his background and experience, I believe that Jared is qualified for the attorney position at your office.

Best,

Laurent

This is an easier and far more persuasive email for an attorney to write. It is different from the other two emails because it can actually be considered a favor *from the working relationship attorney to the hiring attorney*. In other words, because the working-relationship attorney *knows* that you are a strong candidate, the hiring attorney is receiving a benefit by being recommended to hire you. You want emails like this being written on your behalf, and only a working relationship attorney can write them.

The Rule of Reciprocity

The last point to consider on this topic is how to motivate attorneys to help you in the future. Motivating a busy attorney to spend their precious, limited free time furthering your career can be difficult. Certainly, excellent work performance during your internship can increase the chances that attorneys will help you. But this is largely altruistic and relying solely on this notion can be risky. People aren't bad. They are just busy.

Thus, you should keep the Rule of Reciprocity in mind during your internship. When opportunities arise to perform tasks that are not required of you, take advantage. Go above and beyond your typical duties. Help attorneys in any way you can, professionally or personally. Do favors. If asked for a foot, give a yard. This can be anything from staying late, working through the weekend, or simply making copies or grabbing lunch. Be selfless and ask for nothing in return. The well-established Rule of Reciprocity instructs that these attorneys will be inclined to return the favor.

Fostering this dynamic may inspire your assigning attorneys to repay you in the future. Not only can attorneys return favors in meaningful ways (as explained above), but instilling a sense of future obligation can help continue your relationships after the internship ends.

Final Thoughts on Creating Working Relationships with Attorneys

Developing a working relationship with an attorney is not easy; but nothing great ever is. Ensure that your work performance is excellent during your legal internship.

This will help develop relationships. To add some longevity and motivation to the relationship, don't hesitate to go the extra mile for your assigning attorneys. In the end, you will have created a highly beneficial relationship with a practicing attorney who will continue to be a reliable source of guidance, information and recommendations throughout your career.

Chapter 8

DEVELOP AS A PROFESSIONAL

"Without continual growth and progress,
such words as improvement, achievement, and success have no meaning."
Benjamin Franklin

Internships are a goldmine for professional development. By design, internships place you in situations that are unique, dynamic and uncertain. These "stretch experiences" pull you outside of your comfort zone, requiring you to *stretch* yourself further and adapt. *This* is where professional development takes place.

Extensive data published by Michael M. Lombardo, Ed.D., and Robert W. Eichinger, Ph.D., in their book entitled *The Career Architect Development Planner,* established that 70% of professional development occurs **while we are working.** These findings are summarized as follows:

> *Development generally begins with a realization of current or future need and the motivation to do something about it. This might come from feedback, a mistake, watching other people's reactions, failing or not being up to a task — in other words, from experience. The odds are that development will be about 70% from on-the-job experiences, working on tasks and problems; about 20% from feedback and working around good and bad examples of the need; and 10% from courses and reading.*

While working as an intern, you will be thrust into the middle of new, real life matters and asked to problem-solve. You will be surrounded by serious professionals and expected to act like one. Confidences will be shared with you, consequences will flow from the words you speak and write, there will be pressure, deadlines and your work performance will impact real outcomes. All of these situations should lead to profound professional development.

> *Can you think of a time you were stretched outside of your comfort zone in a professional environment? What did it feel like? Were you nervous, anxious or excited? How did you perform in this situation? How did you feel afterwards? Have you since been through that experience for a second time? Did it feel different that second time? Did you feel less nervous? Did your performance improve?*

WHAT IS PROFESSIONAL DEVELOPMENT?

"Professional development" is a vague concept frequently tossed around in conversations. Everybody senses they know what it means, but it is actually quite difficult to define, describe or measure. However, if you are to make quality decisions during law school and achieve a fulfilling career, you must understand why, when and how professional development takes place.

Some professionals develop in a positive way, broadening their capabilities and becoming more dynamic. Others can have minimal or uneven development resulting in job dissatisfaction or a professional plateau. Law students are typically in the beginning stages of professional development, especially within the legal community. Take control of the process. We all develop — but *how* we develop sets us apart from one another.

There are three, interrelated metrics for professional development — (1) professional competency, (2) self-concept and (3) worldview. The opportunity to strengthen and expand these qualities is one of the greatest benefits of an internship.

1. Professional Competency. Professional competency is the combination of knowledge and capability that permits you to perform your job. It has also been described as "situationally-appropriate conduct." Professional competencies are the intangible characteristics that enable you to be efficient, productive, make a positive impression, work well with others and create quality work product. The more professional competencies that you develop, the better attorney you will become.

Lombardo and Eichinger compiled a list of 67 different competencies for leadership development ("Loominger Competencies"). A few examples include:

- approachability
- creativity
- problem-solving
- business acumen
- boss relationships
- composure
- conflict management

In addition, more applicable to legal interns, there is a list of "26 Lawyering Effectiveness Factors" compiled by professors Majorie Schultz and Sheldon Zedeck that were developed to specifically identify the professional competencies that make lawyers successful in their work. Some examples of these factors include:

- Influencing & advocating
- Negotiation skills
- Strategic planning
- Fact finding
- Developing relationships within the legal profession
- Listening

- Practical judgment

On your own, consult the Loominger Competencies and the 26 Lawyering Effectiveness Factors and assess your level in each. This will give you a broad understanding of your strengths and weakness and a starting point for your professional development in this area.

> *What competencies or effectiveness factors do you possess? Are you limited in what you are able to accomplish? What competencies or effectiveness factors have you observed in your colleagues? Supervisors? What specific competencies or effectiveness factors would you like to improve? Which ones do you think are most important?*

2. **Self-Concept.** Your self-concept (or identity) is how you view and evaluate yourself. As an intern surrounded by practicing attorneys, you will constantly be reminded of how little you know. Your work product will need improvement, your opinions will be discounted or discarded and you will attend meetings where you do not understand certain topics and literally say nothing. These moments may be uncomfortable, discouraging or frustrating. But they are also character-building.

Learn who you are in these new, difficult situations without discouragement. Absorb as much information as possible and use the experience to develop your sense of self. This will lead to building your self-esteem, accepting yourself and increasing your ability to engage in accurate, honest and objective self-observation.

> *How would you describe yourself? What are your strengths? Weaknesses? Preferences? What are your core values? Have you ever acted uncharacteristically in an uncomfortable situation? Are you open to feedback or does it sometimes hurt your feelings or cause you to lose confidence? When you critique yourself, how honest are you? Do you sometimes overlook certain shortcomings or make excuses for yourself?*

3. **Worldview.** Your worldview is how you conceive the world. This can include your life philosophy, value systems, emotions and ethical beliefs. Inevitably, we are all influenced by our genetic tendencies, religion, culture and geographic region and past experiences. But with each new experience, our worldview further develops to bring into focus the true nature of reality. We grow to see things for what they really are.

Lawyers are expected to approach situations with complete objectivity. Without bias or misperception, they must see the world for how it really exists in order to render effective advice, take action and solve problems. Working alongside lawyers, the new experiences during your internship will involve matters of high importance, confidential information, shared confidences and interaction with a wide range of individuals and entities. Harness these experiences to develop a well-rounded, well-informed and unbiased worldview to bring reality into focus.

> *How does your worldview differ from those around you? What are your beliefs? Assumptions? Attitudes? Values? What are these based upon? Are you open to changing or expanding how you view the world around you? How has your worldview changed in the last five years?*

Experiences that Lead to Professional Development

Opportunities to develop will be plentiful during your internship. Identifying these moments and understanding how you can develop during them is integral to extracting the most value from your internship and achieving this third overall goal.

The most insightful research studies of professional development have been conducted in the context of leadership development. One of the seminal publications in that field is called *Leader Development: A Review of Research*, by Cynthia McCauley at the Center for Creative Leadership. In that paper, relying on studies from numerous other social psychologists and human resource professionals, McCauley distilled down the following five sources of challenges which, if encountered, are likely to lead to development.

1. Transitions. The entire internship experience is a transition. You leave the hypothetical and academic setting and enter the real world. As an intern, you will have new responsibilities and carry out tasks in which you have little or no familiarity. This new environment will bring new situations, challenges, people and emotions. You will have to stretch yourself to overcome obstacles, identify and understand your emotions and meet these challenges in new and creative ways.

> *Example: You are asked to attend a client meeting and take notes. Many people talk throughout the meeting for a few hours, but you say nothing. Sitting in silence, observing, listening and sometimes not understanding the topic causes you to question the value you are bringing to the meeting. This train of thought causes you to lose focus on the conversation and become insecure about whether other people are noticing that you said nothing.*

This is not an uncommon situation for an intern to find themselves in. In these moments, it is imperative that you become aware of your emotions, rely on your sense of self for reassurance that you *are* valuable and remember that your role is not to talk, but rather to listen and take notes. If this is something you have difficulty with, do not judge yourself. Just acknowledge it as an area of professional development that needs improvement.

2. Fostering Change. There is often no clear path to follow when practicing law. Thus, attorneys are constantly dealing with uncertainty as they enter a situation and take affirmative steps to alter the circumstances. But when faced with ambiguity, attorneys are expected to remain focused and find solutions. As an intern, you will be expected to do the same as you participate in transactions, assist with unpredictable litigations and generally navigate the day to day challenges in a law office. You will consistently witness the unraveling of the action and reaction process.

> Example: *You are asked to review thousands of pages of documents, make copies and enter the information on those documents into an excel spreadsheet as part of a damages analysis. While you are making copies, the copying machine breaks down and you spend an entire morning trying to fix it. Then, after numerous hours of entering the data into the excel document, you realize that early in the project you made an error that caused the entire analysis to be inaccurate. These two issues cause you to fall far behind in the assignment and make it impossible to meet your deadline.*

When you started the assignment, you may have thought that everything would go smoothly. But you have now learned that things rarely go smoothly and there are always issues that arise. This is a reality that has now become part of your more-developed worldview. In dealing with your own mistake and subsequently communicating the bad news to your assigning attorney, you will have developed many professional competencies such as boss relationships, composure, command skills, conflict management, directing others and organizing. You will have also learned that you need to improve your attention to detail.

3. **High Levels of Responsibility.** If an intern successfully earns the trust of a supervisor, the intern may be charged with performing a meaningful function from which real consequences flow. This is an enviable place to be. But it is also a complicated one, where the intern's performance is highly visible and the pressure is great.

> Example: *Your assigning attorney is out of the office and calls you to electronically file a document in federal court. He is not present to oversee the filing but explains the process. You do some independent research to ensure you understand the procedure fully. Then you file it successfully. The assigning attorney and the client are pleased with your work.*

Something as seemingly simple as a court filing is a task that may actually be complicated and has real consequences. If done incorrectly, deadlines may get missed and rights of the parties may be prejudiced. Being entrusted with this high level responsibility required you to think strategically, perform well under pressure, prioritize and make tough decisions with limited oversight. Such an experience strengthens your self-concept and further develops numerous professional competencies, such as learning on the fly, personal learning and problem-solving.

4. **Influencing People.** Do not underestimate how important it is to be liked by your colleagues. Interns work *for* attorneys; but they work *with* the support staff. Interns may have no authority over other professionals, but nonetheless need their help. While an intern may have legal acumen and higher education, they are only a temporary employee. Support staff, on the other hand, may be older, more professionally experienced, and may have a long tenure at the organization. An intern should build relationships with their support staff and peers, communicate effectively with and motivate them.

> Example: *Your assigning attorney asks you to create multiple exhibit binders for a trial. But you do not know where to get the binders, how to perform*

certain functions on the copy machine, where the hole-puncher is or how to locate exhibit tabs, stamps, stickers, markers and labels. The office services employee is much older than you, somewhat grumpy and constantly complains about being overworked. Yet, you need their help to get the assignment done. The assigning attorney tells you that it needs to be done quickly and must be "perfect."

Your main challenge in this situation will be to motivate the office services employee to help you. But you must also communicate that the assignment needs to be done quickly and with no mistakes. Your communication style must be direct and assertive, not passive aggressive or overly aggressive. You must be sensitive to their mood, ego and how they view you, while keeping in mind that it is the work product, not individual needs, that is of highest importance. This type of interaction is highly difficult and misunderstandings can lead to poor work product. But as you progress through it, you will develop your interpersonal savvy, managerial courage and patience — all crucial professional competencies for an attorney.

5. Dealing with Diversity. The legal profession attracts individuals from various backgrounds, genders, ethnicities and origins. People will be different ages, have different educational backgrounds, have different communication styles, physical appearances and have different cultures. In order to collaborate effectively with a diverse group of professionals, interns must respect other's value systems, challenge and crystallize their own beliefs and assimilate multiple perspectives.

Example: Your assigning attorney is extremely abrasive and difficult to work for. He speaks loudly and quickly, is demanding and provides virtually no positive feedback. On one occasion, he meets with you to review a memorandum that you wrote and spends the entire time criticizing your writing style, pointing out the issues that you failed to identify and tells you to write it again. When you try to ask him a question, he loses his patience, says that he is late for another meeting and leaves. You now go back to your desk and are worried about going through that experience again.

Not all supervising attorneys or co-workers will be a pleasure to work with. Lawyers work under pressure, navigate tight deadlines, deal with matters implicating a significant amount of money and personal liberties and may overlook typical pleasantries that are common in other work environments. Your ability to manage your own anxiety, seek out alternative resources to assist in your work, communicate effectively and get the job done under these circumstances will present a lofty challenge. Regardless of whether you succeed or fail, these experiences where you deal with diverse and sometimes difficult personalities will strengthen your professional competency, open your eyes to the realities of the legal profession and further solidify your sense of self.

Undoubtedly, stretch experiences are challenging. But you must resist the tendency to go into "survival mode" during these times. Instead, embrace the challenge. As Eckhart Tolle teaches, in *The Power of Now*, you should "be present" and experience each moment as it happens. Incorporate this philosophy into your work. Pay attention to your actions, reactions and those of the people around you. This will make your development more profound and deep.

Your performance during these challenging situations will serve as starting points for your professional development. And in the end, you will have *expanded* your comfort zone — the essence of growth through experience.

> *In what ways are you developed? Underdeveloped? How well were you able to understand your co-worker's perspective? How well do you work with different personality types? Genders? Ethnic backgrounds? Are there certain types of people with whom you prefer to work? Are you uncomfortable dealing with uncertainty? Did you enjoy working independently? How does support staff respond to your instructions? Are you calm under pressure?*

Final Thoughts on Professional Development

Your professional development is a foundation for all that you accomplish and, for that reason, it is perhaps the most important of all three internship goals. Through your stretch experiences and the development of your professional competencies, self-identity and worldview, you will begin to see the professional world around you with increasing clarity. Reality will reveal itself. What is important will come into focus and, at the same time, you will have the maturity to seize it. Your legal internship is a crucial opportunity during law school to accelerate your professional development.

PART IV:

PERFORMANCE DURING YOUR INTERNSHIP

Once you've landed your internship and locked in your goals, it is time to shift your mindset to one word — performance. All of your introspectiveness and aspirations will amount to very little if you cannot meet the challenges that your internship will present. You're done thinking and talking about being lawyer. It is now time to demonstrate to yourself and the organization that you can perform like a lawyer. It is game time.

This Part IV is dedicated to performance during your internship. It opens with an overview of how to prepare for the first day of your internship. After that, you will learn about the five central components to successful performance during your legal internship — enthusiasm, attention to detail, stress management, upward management of your supervising attorneys, and nailing your legal research assignments. The Part then finishes with a review of twenty tips for successful performance and how to bring your internship to a close.

Chapter 9

PREPARE FOR YOUR INTERNSHIP

Now that you've obtained and set goals for your internship, put aside some time preparing to hit the ground running on day one. True, the unpredictable nature of an internship experience does limit the ways to prepare and much of your success will depend on your ability to think on your feet and perform. That being said, here are a few ways to get a head start.

Research the Organization

Just as you would research a foreign land that you were soon to visit, you should study your new workplace before the first day. The more you know about your internship organization beforehand, the better equipped you will be to achieve success upon arrival.

You should have already done some research during the application process. But now that you know for certain where you will be working, go back to conduct further research and learn much as you can about:

The Organization's Background. Every organization has a history. Learn when it was started, how it was created, its founder(s), its mission, assets, growth and any changes it has experienced throughout its existence. These pieces of information will help you assimilate to the organization's culture, understand what it values the most, and connect with its leaders.

> *Law firm considerations: Does the founder partner(s) have a unique background? For example, he/she left a large firm as an associate to go out on his/her own, you can anticipate that the firm (and at least the managing partner) will value entrepreneurial spirit. Learn the firm's practice areas and the specific services that each one provides. Has the firm grown since its inception? When was it founded?*
>
> *In-house considerations: Inquire into the financial health of the company (check the Securities and Exchange Commission website if publicly-traded). Also check out its brands, divisions, structure, affiliates, trademarks or other assets such as real estate holdings. Has it undergone any recent organizational changes like a merger, purchase, IPO? Who are the competitors and how does the company differentiate itself? What is the state of the industry?*
>
> *Non-profit considerations: Understand the organization's mission. Is it based on a particular philosophy or research study? Does the organization have corporate partners? Who are its founders? What is their background? Is the organization privately funded or does it receive government money? What*

is the structure of the organization? Who sits on the board of directors? Who runs its committees?

Government considerations: When was the organization created? Was it launched by one or more politicians or judges? What is/was their background? Was the organization created to solve a problem or in response to an event? How is it funded? How could a political shift impact its growth/contracting? What is the organization's structure? What is that organization's overall place in the larger political context? What kinds of incentives does the organization respond to? Quotas? Objectives? Stakeholders? How does the organization measure success? Key players and who they report to?

Current Events. Organizations are constantly reacting and adapting to external forces which can impact the overall morale, working conditions, future, identity or outlook of the organization. To help understand and interpret these conditions when you arrive, you should be apprised of recent issues the organization is encountering such as recent cases, legislation, political shifts, organizational successes/failures, technological changes, new hires or trends in the industry.

Law firm considerations: If a law firm recently won a large jury verdict, be sure to read that decision, understand the issues in that case and be prepared to discuss it during the internship.

In-house considerations: If a company has experienced layoffs and budgetary cuts due to a shift in the industry, you should research the economics behind that change and be aware of how this recent development may impact company morale and your prospects for getting hired permanently. If your internship is at a highly-regulated company, look into current and upcoming public policy changes that may impact the organization.

Non-profit considerations: If the non-profit recently received a large grant to expand and open an office in a new city, you should research why they received the grant, for what purpose the money should be used, how it may impact staffing and potential opportunities at the new office.

Government considerations: If the EEOC recently received a directive from the White House to pursue systemic discrimination for large corporations, research the thought/reasons behind the directive and how it may impact the projects you'll have during the internship.

Knowledge is power. Don't start your internship naïve about what matters to the organization. The more you learn about the organization, the more effective you will be demonstrating your alignment with its mission, demystifying your work environment, building relationships with its people and navigating office politics.

How and Where to Research

For objective facts, first turn to electronic and print materials. But keep in mind that the information that organizations publish about themselves are intended to portray a certain image. You should read organizational websites and press releases with a certain amount of skepticism. In many instances, the best objective information can be acquired from third-party sources such as trade publications and websites, law review articles, market analyses and the like.

There is also valuable "inside" information that is best acquired through word of mouth. Look to your network for contacts or weak contacts who might have first-hand information about your internship organization. Check with alumni, bar association contacts, friends/relatives, legal recruiters or headhunters, or other former interns or employees from the organization. People are the best and sometimes only source of information about the culture of an organization, the personalities or preferences of particular attorneys, the organization's reputation or other unwritten information.

Research Your Role

Try to anticipate your role during your internship and gather as much information as possible to boost your competence and confidence on day one, in this role.

Center your role-specific research on the following questions:

1. Will my internship focus in a particular practice area? If so, which one(s)? Each practice area has certain statutes, regulations, codes and/or seminal case law decisions with which all attorneys in that practice area must be familiar. Research and identify these central authorities and understand them. Then read treatises or law review articles that discuss these materials to provide perspective on how they are generally viewed in the profession, how they have changed over time and potential changes in the future.

> *For example: If you anticipate assisting in state or federal court litigation matters, be sure to familiarize yourself with the court systems and applicable procedural rules. Review a practice management guide focusing in litigation in that jurisdiction and be sure that you know the proper citation format that will be used.*

2. Will my internship focus in a particular geographic region? If so, which one(s)? Each geographic area has delineated jurisdictions, court systems, agencies, political districts, municipal bodies, regulators, and other government entities that create and enforce the laws. Regardless of whether you practice in the private or public sector, all attorneys must be familiar and work with the government in their geographic area. Research and identify these different government bodies, their missions, how they may impact your internship organization and any other information that may assist in understanding how attorneys view these organizations.

> *For example: If you anticipate working on criminal defense matters in New York City, you should familiarize yourself with the various agencies and organizations that you might encounter, such as the criminal justice services, probation departments, correctional facilities, public defender agencies, police departments, the different criminal courts and the judges presiding over each, the prosecutors' offices, attorney general offices, county sheriffs, or rehabilitation facilities. Understand each organization's jurisdiction, mission, structure, and whether they have their own individual procedural rules/guidelines. You can get most of this information from their websites and news articles.*

3. Will there be a specific project/case that I am assigned to? If so, what is it? Often times, an intern may spend their entire internship working in a supporting role on a single project, deal, lawsuit or article. If this will be your situation, then research all important aspects of that matter and try to become an expert. Each project will have an industry, a client, opposing counsel, a specific practice area, sub-practice area and associated legal issues. Become familiar with this background information ahead of time.

> *For example:* *If you know that one of your main internship projects with be assisting the in-house counsel negotiate leases on multiple residential units of a newly-acquired building, then you should do some extra research on how to negotiate a lease, typical clauses and issues, real estate, landlord/tenant, land use and housing discrimination laws that may apply, the government agencies that inspect and regulate residential apartments, and the housing court system.*

If you don't know enough about your anticipated role to adequately prepare, consider reaching out to your future supervising attorney and ask questions about what he/she plans to have you do. Then use this information to guide your research. If the supervising attorney appears receptive, ask them what he/she thinks that you should be doing to prepare.

Starting your internship with this background knowledge will send the message that you are enthusiastic and invested in success. It will also reduce the amount of time that your supervising attorney will have to spend getting you up to speed in a particular area. This, in turn, will enable you to boost the office's productivity quicker.

ANTICIPATE AND ADDRESS POTENTIAL CHALLENGES

If you expect to experience difficulty in a particular aspect of your internship, don't shy away from this fact. Take it head on and do as much preparation as possible to minimize or eliminate this potential difficulty. Some sources of difficulties may include:

• ***Lacking relevant general experience.*** Go back to your resumé and the job description. Were you missing any general experiences that the organization identified as relevant to the position? If so, try to compensate for this by doing some extra research to get you up to speed.

> *For example:* *Your internship may be at a law firm and you have no prior experience working in a law firm. If this is your situation, you should research — generally — how law firms function, their purpose, billing practices and their structure to get yourself up to speed on this new organization type.*

• ***Lacking relevant specific experience.*** Are there any skills that the organization emphasized during the application process that you are weak in or lack completely? If so, engage in some independent skill-building exercises to raise your competency level.

> *For example:* *You may anticipate performing damages calculations in Microsoft Excel in connection with a specific litigation project. If you have no*

prior experience using Excel, you should take an online course, watch some YouTube videos, or buy a workbook to learn the basics before your internship begins.

- ***Prior difficulty in certain tasks.*** Do you have any recurring issues with your work performance that you anticipate may arise again during this upcoming internship? If so, do some upfront work to ensure that history does not repeat itself.

For example: You may have struggled in the past with your organizational skills and anticipate that your internship will involve a high level of multitasking and juggling multiple assignments at once. You should research organization strategies and systems and/or purchase and practice using an organizational tool, such as a planner.

Everybody has unique strengths and weaknesses. What separates the good from the great is the ability to identify and improve on the weaknesses. Be honest with yourself about your shortcomings and address them ahead of time to ensure that they don't become unmanageable and/or negatively impact your work performance.

Learn Your Learning Style

People have different ways which they absorb and interpret information to learn new skills. Your internship will likely be a whirlwind of learning opportunities. If you haven't already, evaluate your learning style to position yourself to learn as much as possible:

- **Are you an auditory learner?** Do you learn best by hearing and listening? If so, you will be predisposed to learn a great deal through active observation of your supervising attorneys, discussions, conferences and brainstorming sessions.
- **Are you a visual learner?** Do you learn best by reading? If so, you may find that you learn the most while engaging in abstract conceptualism/ independent research in between performing your assignments.
- **Are you an active/tactile learner?** Do you learn best by doing? If so, concrete experiences when you are actually performing your assignments may be the moments of greatest benefit during your internship.
- **Are you a reflective learner?** Do you learn best when you sit back and think through your experiences? If so, you may gravitate towards and gain the most value from engaging in your internal discourses after each assignment.

Think about your preferred learning environment and situations where you excelled in absorbing and applying new information. If you are unsure or curious about your learning style, take an assessment test. The more you understand about your learning style, the more control you will have over your learning during your internship.

Figure Out Logistics

Your first impression is key. You don't want to be experiencing personal difficulties the first day, week or month of work at your internship. Be sure to research any and all aspects of the commute and parking situation. Perhaps take a test run to reduce stress and the possibility of arriving late. If you are moving to a new geographic area for your internship, be proactive to ensure that you obtain a stable, reliable and tranquil living situation. These types of outside-of-the-office issues can disrupt your work performance at a critical time period in your internship.

Identify Networking Opportunities

Your upcoming internship is the newest chapter of your story, which may plug you into a new community, practice area, organization-type or location. Assess how your network may have expanded through this new position and identify any individuals who may be new potential contacts or weak contacts. If it makes sense, send out some emails and try to set up informational interviews during your internship.

Chapter 10

BE ENTHUSIASTIC

Starting on day one and continuing for every minute of your internship, you should be enthusiastic. This mentality must become ingrained into your work personality and underlie everything you do. Enthusiasm is a necessary trait for *any* successful professional, so it is particularly important for you to exhibit during your internship, as you develop positive work habits and sculpt your professional persona. It may sound simple, but remaining consistently and genuinely enthusiastic throughout an internship may actually be quite difficult.

The Benefits of Being Enthusiastic

Enthusiasm is the fuel that brings about positive outcomes. It can help you engage for longer periods of time, maintain focus, increase productivity and spur better ideas and imaginative, innovative methods to achieving results. When you're enthusiastic, you'll reflexively devote more time and energy to your assignments and go beyond what is expected of you. And perhaps most rewarding of all, genuine enthusiasm enhances your enjoyment of the work and overall job satisfaction.

An enthusiastic approach to your work will also yield numerous external benefits during your internship. For example, your enthusiasm can positively impact your situation by:

- Lifting the spirits of your co-workers and making the office a more pleasant place to be. Interns can be a welcomed and refreshing source of enthusiasm.
- Giving off positive energy and influencing the people in your office to be around and work with you, which makes for a more collaborative experience.
- Inviting attorneys to give you more and different kinds of challenging assignments, which leads to gaining more practical skills, transfer of more tacit knowledge, solidifying working relationships with attorneys and furthering professional development.
- Conveying the message that you are invested in achieving positive outcomes for the organization, which encourages attorneys to trust your ability to generate quality work product.

Most importantly, displaying genuine enthusiasm for your work motivates assigning attorneys *to invest in you.* They may spend more time explaining the background of an assignment, their strategic thinking, insights on the practice area, career guidance and/or giving tailored, thoughtful feedback on your performance.

Case Study: You're helping an attorney prepare for a deposition. She asks you to stay late to make copies, compile and index exhibits and create binders. It is a time-consuming, secretarial-like task and the assigning attorney knows it. But you don't care about that. You stay focused on the importance of your work, ask thoughtful questions when appropriate and never express any disappointment or hesitation about staying late. The attorney notices and appreciates your enthusiasm.

After the deposition concludes the next day, you have questions about the attorney's strategy, the line of questioning and some of the deposition procedures. Because she appreciated your assistance the night before and recognized your unwavering enthusiasm for the work, she sits with you and spends an hour "de-briefing" about the deposition and answers all of your questions. This creates an enhanced learning experience for you, strengthens your relationship with the attorney and helps cement your acquisition of skills. The attorney may not have spent that hour with you if she thought that you weren't invested in the work. Your enthusiastic approach swayed her to invest in you.

On the flipside, attorneys are usually quite sensitive to when an intern appears unenthusiastic, unappreciative or distracted. Giving off these vibes during your internship can convey the wrong message and cause assigning attorneys to become disinterested, distrusting or even resentful towards you. Regardless of what you are experiencing internally, externally you must communicate nothing other than absolute enthusiasm for your work. But, as illustrated below, this may be easier said than done.

Challenges to Being Enthusiastic

Obviously, it is easier to be enthusiastic during your internship when you are assigned important "real" work and receive positive feedback, encouragement, support and recognition from your supervising attorneys. If this is your internship environment, then your level of enthusiasm will likely be a non-issue.

However, your internship may throw some curveballs at you that challenge your ability to stay positive, outwardly enthusiastic and internally motivated to get the job done. Here are a few issues that interns commonly encounter:

1. Difficult Work Environment. Interns typically inherit the least attractive office locations and resources such as low-functioning computers, software or telephones, isolated work stations in the basement, different floors or unpopulated wings of an office, poor lighting, or uncomfortable chairs. These working conditions can frustrate your ability to get your work done and send the message that you're not important to or valued by the organization.

2. Insignificant Assignments. It is not uncommon for interns to be given the repetitive document review project, the mindless gopher assignment delivering/picking up documents or to sit in a meeting and say absolutely nothing. It is also usual for interns to create work product that is not reviewed until weeks later, if ever. These types of assignments may make you feel diminished and that there is little consequence to your work.

3. Minimal Direction. Interns are sometimes given assignments from attorneys in a way that impedes their ability to get the job done. For instance, you may not be given adequate background information or the necessary resources to get the work done. And when you have questions, the assigning attorney is not always available to answer them. You go back to your desk riddled with confusion and frustration, feel completely lost and unable to get the work done.

4. **Tough Supervisors.** Not all supervising attorneys are going to be kind. Particularly in a stressful work environment, attorneys can be terse, rude and/or condescending. They may exhibit a complete disinterest in your feelings and lack of common courtesy. Yet, you may be required to do what they say, when they say to do it. It can be difficult working for someone who treats you poorly.

5. **No Feedback.** Feedback is a luxury during an internship. Attorneys are usually quite busy and they may not see any benefit to spending their precious time explaining what you did wrong, what you did right, and how to improve. If this is your situation and you are unable to facilitate any feedback, then you may feel lost about the quality of your work product and areas of improvement.

6. **Stressful Situations.** In circumstances when assignments are piling up on your desk, deadlines are rapidly approaching and your supervisors are exuding anxiety, you may want to scream, run away, or hide under your desk. Being overwhelmed and stressed out can put you into survival mode and remove all enjoyment from the work.

7. **Overwork.** Some offices may be understaffed and ask you to do the work of two or three interns. You may have multiple attorneys giving you time-sensitive assignments without communicating with each other. You may be consistently coming in early, working late, cancelling personal plans, and working through weekends. You may start feeling unappreciated or burnt out.

8. **Unachievable assignments.** Interns are frequently given the "needle-in-the-haystack" research assignments where they are asked to locate some non-existent case. These types of assignments position you for failure, and it can be demoralizing to constantly be reporting back to attorneys that you were unable to find a case or solve a problem.

Don't let these difficult circumstances get the best of you and impede you from maintaining an enthusiastic approach to your job. Be resilient and look inward to garner a self-starting mentality. Stoke up your intrinsic motivation to overcome negative external forces and ensure that, no matter what, you outwardly display genuine enthusiasm for the job.

> <u>Side Note:</u> While you should certainly attempt to overcome adversity through your own inner strength and resources, as a law student, you are never alone in this experience. If your internship is presenting an overwhelming amount of challenges, reach out to trusted professionals at your school to help brainstorm a plan for effectively approaching and improving your situation. Often times, an extra perspective on a difficult situation can help bring much needed clarity.

Be Intrinsically Motivated

Genuine enthusiasm begins from the inside out. Each day you arrive at the office, you must make a conscious decision not just to *act* excited and interested about your work, but to actually *be* this way. Adopt a positive outlook towards your role. Search for the aspects of your job that you appreciate. Identify how your work fits into the big picture. Hone in on what really matters to you and the organization and incorporate these objectives into your current assignment.

To foster your intrinsic motivation during your internship, especially during challenging times, try reaffirming and reminding yourself that:

- The organization hired you because they believe that you can get the job done well. You have the intelligence, skills and work ethic to contribute real value.
- Your individual assignments are important, even if that importance is not readily apparent or explained to you.
- Your role at the organization is to provide critical support and do all that is asked of you to further the organization's mission. You must embrace this supporting role before you can ascend to other positions.
- Every work assignment is a valuable opportunity to learn, expand or improve your practical legal skills, create or strengthen your working relationships and/or develop as a professional. Work assignments are the vehicle to advance your career. The more work, the more strides you make down your career path.
- All practical legal skills, large or small, are important to gain. Each time you are performing a task, no matter how mundane it may appear, you are building your skill sets and investing in yourself.
- If someone treats you poorly without a reason, it likely has to do with their situation, not yours. Don't take it personally or let their "stuff" get in the way of you doing your job.
- All experiences, especially frustrating or difficult ones, accelerate professional and personal growth. Your most difficult experiences may actually be the most beneficial.
- Each time an attorney gives you feedback, even if it is harsh or seemingly unfair, they are investing in your career. Don't focus on the delivery. Focus on the content and message, and how to use the information to improve.

These are just some examples of ways to keep yourself motivated and enthusiastic about your work regardless of what is going on around you. Connecting with your intrinsic motivation is the key to deriving meaning and fulfillment from your job.

> *Example Case Study:* *During your internship, you spend one month involved in a trial. You sense that there are many fascinating factual and legal issues involving the trial, but you don't come anywhere near working on those issues. Instead, during this time, your job consists entirely of making copies of hundreds of pages of exhibits, marking the documents with exhibit tabs, creating an index and organizing the documents into folders that would be*

pulled during direct and cross examination. You spend tens of hours each day making copies, essentially a secretarial task. At times, you become frustrated with the monotony and discouraged at how unimportant your role appears. You also work long nights and weekends isolated in the copy room. This is a difficult place for you to be, as you are eager to hone your legal skills through research, writing and discussing the legal issues in the trial.

But you remain focused on the task you are given and seek ways to uncover the value in your work. While there is nothing interesting about making copies, you find that the way you organized and labeled the exhibits would be important at trial. You ask questions as to how the exhibits would be introduced and use this information to design the way you organized them. Internally, you draw logical, causal connections between the presentation of exhibits to the effectiveness of witness questioning, persuasiveness of evidence and, ultimately, whether or not your team would be successful at trial. You find a way to link your boring, somewhat mindless task to a very important outcome. Revealing the importance of the work made it easier to be enthusiastic. Being enthusiastic helped you enjoy the work and improved your work product.

Ways to Communicate Your Enthusiasm

Being genuinely enthusiastic towards your work may not get you anywhere if you are unable to communicate this feeling to your assigning attorneys and co-workers. Here are a few tips for displaying your enthusiasm:

- <u>Smile:</u> This is the first and most obvious tip. Bring a cheerful attitude to every one-on-one meeting with attorneys, group meetings, presentations to clients, networking events or any other venues where your co-workers will observe your professional behavior and representation of the organization. Being serious about your work does not mean you cannot smile.
- <u>Express appreciation:</u> There is nothing wrong or awkward about saying "thank you" to an attorney after they give you an assignment or critical feedback on your work. They are spending their precious time focused on your experience and improvement. Let them know you appreciate it.
- <u>Take the extra step:</u> Legal work is complex and there is always extra research or details to be explored before reaching absolute certainty. Keep an eye out for unanswered questions or opportunities for further research on an issue. Take initiative and do this extra work without being asked. This will bring value to a project, impress your assigning attorney and show that you are invested in the outcome.
- <u>Make room for work:</u> Exhibit a willingness to take on more work. Volunteer to help a colleague with their work. Stretch your work capacity as far as you can and, when you have gone too far, seek advice on how to handle it. Being fully engaged is key. This will make you an indispensable asset to the organization.

- Show passion: Just because this is a job does not mean you cannot be personally invested. As an intern, you are a visitor in the office. But the attorneys live and breathe these matters, sometimes for years. They care. If you want to connect with them on that level, feel free to display your passion for the work.
- Be forward thinking: Don't just be a problem-identifier, be a problem-solver. Be forward thinking about your assignments and, if the opportunity presents itself, express suggestions for resolution. If you uncover through legal research that there are obstacles, start a conversation about how to overcome those obstacles. Be vocal about your desire to find solutions. It's not about what happened in the past; it's about what to do next.
- Stay positive through adversity: It is easy to stay excited about your work when things are going well. The true test of your enthusiasm towards your work will occur when you encounter adversity. You misplace a document. Opposing counsel refuses to consent. A deadline is quick approaching. Show your co-workers that you are genuinely and deeply enthusiastic, regardless of the circumstances.
- Seek out personal interaction: Don't be a hermit. Get up from your desk, visit other people's offices, or ask them out to lunch. Spend energy getting to know your co-workers. Part of practicing law is working with people. Be enthusiastic about your co-workers and work environment.
- Don't be negative: Don't complain about anything, plain and simple. Limit bringing up your personal life or problems. Everybody has issues in their personal life; it can be unprofessional to talk about them at work.
- Be inquisitive: Expressing an interest, asking questions, and digging to the bottom of problems are all ways to demonstrate and fuel your own enthusiasm.

In the end, when you are enthusiastic, it impacts you and everyone around you. Others will pick up on your enthusiasm, may even become excited themselves and then feed your enthusiasm back to you. It can become a beautiful circle of energy.

Chapter 11

DEMONSTRATE A STRONG ATTENTION TO DETAIL

Possessing a strong attention to detail requires no special talent or contribution from someone else. It is an utterly solitary endeavor and entirely within your control. Thus, you can and should develop this positive trait and showcase it throughout their internship. It is the foundation of excellent work performance of every intern and attorney.

The Importance of Attention to Detail

Attention to detail, in its most basic sense, is the achievement of thoroughness and accuracy when accomplishing a task through concern for all of the areas involved. It means to take care in every task that you perform. During your internship, your attention to detail (or lack thereof) will likely be challenged in the following ways:

- Grammar: Avoiding grammatical, typographical, formatting and spelling errors in your writing and when asked to find and fix such errors in others' work-product.
- Math: Putting together mathematical calculations that are complete and accurate.
- Organization: Organizing and compiling documents, exhibits, contracts, riders, schedules, binders, research or other voluminous written materials that are in the correct order and not missing pages or sections.
- Time Management: Arriving to meetings, conference calls, appointments, court appearances or other important events on time (or early), in the correct location and fully prepared to participate or assist the attorney in their participation. This also includes allotting sufficient time to meet deadlines to submit work-product to the assigning attorney, such as research assignments or drafting memoranda, letters, court documents or contracts.
- Specifics: Reciting accurate information pertaining to dates, times, names, addresses, events, locations, numbers or other specific details that are important to a particular matter.
- Following direction: Performing tasks precisely in the manner, procedure or order in which you are instructed by your assigning attorney.

You should strive for your attention to detail in these areas to be perfect. As an intern, you are not expected to know the law, facts, strategy or demonstrate an attorney-level aptitude for solving problems. However, you will be expected to have a strong attention to detail in these above areas.

Failing in this regard can be costly. Missing details can erode trust and damage working relationships, reduce the office's efficiency and limit your internship experience.

> <u>*Case Study:*</u> *You are given an assignment to prepare a folder for an attorney's court appearance to argue a motion. You are instructed to create a folder with copies of all motion papers and annexed exhibits. You do this, but rush through it because of another assignment with an approaching deadline. You don't do a final review of all of the documents. When the attorney gets the court, one of the exhibits to the motion, a contract, is missing from the folder and the attorney is unable to quote a provision to the judge. This diminishes the oral argument. That attorney, at the least, will likely have lost trust for you and will have to double-check all the work you do in the future, thereby limiting your level of responsibility. At the worst, that attorney may be upset and decide not to work with you again, thereby limiting your work assignments and opportunities to learn and develop.*

Don't let this happen to you. Be sure to rely on your attention to detail as the foundation for each and every assignment that you perform.

How to Demonstrate Attention to Detail

Exhibiting strong attention to detail is a somewhat hidden accomplishment that rarely yields praise. Nobody is going to say: "Wow, her memorandum had no typos in it," "Wow, she was on time for that meeting," or "Wow, there were no pages missing from the exhibits and they were all in order." As a matter of course, your work performance and product should always be error-free. This is the baseline expectation.

It may be possible that the only time your attention to detail will be noticed is when you *miss a detail.* Rest assured, if a page is missing from a contract, your sentence has a double-period at the end, or if you're late or unprepared, it will be noticed and remembered. And it will not reflect positively on you in the moment or on your overall reputation.

There is, however, one way in which you can achieve positive recognition for your attention to detail — that is, support your co-workers/assigning attorneys by helping them be perfect. If done tactfully, this can be an effective way of becoming an indispensable member of the team. As a few examples, you may:

- Catch and fix a factual or grammatical error in a supervising attorney's work product;
- Send a reminder to a supervising attorney about an upcoming meeting or deadline; or
- Have specific documents or details on-hand without being asked, such as the phone number of opposing counsel or a print-out of an important case.

Your role is to provide support. Don't battle this reality — embrace it. Your supervisors will appreciate your contribution and think of you as someone who is reliable and engaged in their work, no matter how tedious the task. Gaining such a positive reputation is a big benefit derived from a very small action.

> Side Note: Highlighting/fixing an attorney's mistakes or reminding them of deadlines must be done in a delicate way, especially if you are doing it on your own volition and without being asked. Be careful not to come off as pretentious or annoying. Therefore, always provide this type of support in the spirit of teamwork, not individual achievement. Your tone, words and actions must communicate that it is not about ego, it is only about getting the job done correctly.

Typical Intern Errors

Interns usually commit the same kinds of repeat errors due to lack of attention to detail. It may be that they feel rushed to submit an assignment or have poor habits or systems. Either way, keep a lookout for these common intern mistakes that are avoidable simply by heightening your attention to detail:

- Submitting written documents (emails, memoranda, letters, etc.) with typos, grammatical errors, spelling errors or mathematical errors.

  Tip — Whenever you feel that you are done drafting a letter, email or memo, read it one more time aloud. This tends to catch the "gremlins" that creep into our writing. And, double then triple-check your math.

- Submitting materials with factual inaccuracies such as a person's name, contact information, title, address, dates, times, etc.

  Tip — Don't rely on memory. Cross-reference and double check specific facts and spelling with your notes or primary sources to ensure that it is correct.

- Submitting memoranda with inaccurate citations to legal authority and use of quotations.

  Tip - Re-read a quotation to make sure that each comma, period, contraction, or minute details are recited perfectly in your memo. Pretend that you are a stranger picking up your memo for the first time and confirm that your citation points to the correct portion of the case/statute.

- Being late for or missing a meeting entirely, whether inter-office or at another location, or missing deadlines.

  Tip — Whenever you're invited to a meeting or given a deadline, write it down, circle it and put it in your calendar as soon as you get back to your desk. Don't proceed forward with anything else until these important dates/times are out of your brain and in your calendar.

- Submitting multi-page documents/exhibits that have missing pages, are mis-numbered, or out of order.

  Tip — When you feel that you are ready to submit your work product, commit additional time to flipping through and putting your eyes on every page.

- Writing an email referencing an attachment, but failing to attach the actual document.

  Tip — Make a habit of every time you are about to hit send on an email, reading it one more time. And, you should always open up each attachment and scroll through the entire document to make sure no pages are missing. This habit will ensure that you catch if the attachment is missing entirely, or is an incomplete document.

In addition, there is one intern mistake that is so common that it deserves a more lengthy description - making errors when using forms, templates, or modifying other documents.

> *Case Study Assignment:* *You are asked to draft a Stipulation of Dismissal and told to use a stipulation from a different lawsuit as a template. If you fail to pay close enough attention to the details in the text, you may forget to change the date, signature block, index number, caption, court, the number of parties ("defendant" or "defendants") or other details specific to your matter.*

There is something about working off of another document that lures an intern into being lazy, rushing through the assignment and not proofreading thoroughly. It is best for you to be aware of this trap before your internship so you don't make this extremely common intern mistake. These types of mistakes can plague interns and can have many negative consequences, such as:

- A grammatical error can change the entire meaning of a sentence.
- A mathematical error can result in lost profits for a client.
- Missing a deadline can be (and likely will be) *per se* malpractice.
- Even small, seemingly-unimportant typos can leave a negative impression on a judge or signal weakness to an adversary.

The stakes are high for a practicing attorney. You must hold yourself to the same standards of excellence and ensure that your work-product is perfect.

How to Improve Your Attention to Detail

Your internship is a great time to implement positive habits that strengthen your attention to detail. You can practice new methods in real time, test what works for you, and notice as your work product and performance become more reliable as a result. Don't be nervous. Everybody makes mistakes. Do your best to make as few as possible. Here are some tips to accomplish this:

1. Devote equal energy to drafting and proofreading. When given a writing assignment, think of drafting and proofreading as two distinct stages both deserving of equal attention. If you finish a first draft and are mentally fatigued, don't jump right into proofreading with low focus and energy. Step away from the assignment for a while until you are re-energized and prepared to devote your full attention to proofreading.

2. Be a hypercritical of your work product. Readers of legal writing are typically skeptical and have an eye to judge. Beat them to the punch. Be hypercritical of your work product before anyone else is. Crank down to an excruciating level of detail and focus on the minutia. Obsess over spacing, formatting, punctuation, word tense, citations and spelling. No detail is too small.

3. Proofread everything. Obviously, you should proofread all drafts of letters, memoranda, contracts, affidavits, pleadings, motion papers, damages calculations, or other documents that are submitted to courts, adversaries or other attorneys. But also be sure to apply this same level of scrutiny to your internal and external emails or other less formal writings, regardless of the anticipated recipient. You never know where your work-product will end up. Make sure it is perceived as flawless wherever it goes.

4. Break down tasks into smaller ones. Tackling a massive, long-term or multi-faceted assignment can be overwhelming, make you feel perpetually behind, like you're not making progress, or provoke you to rush. If you feel this happening, identify logical places to break the assignment down into sub-assignments. By narrowing your focus, you will reduce anxiety, take your time, and catch more mistakes.

5. Increase interest. This ties into being enthusiastic. If you are interested and invested in your work, and connected with its bigger purpose, you can focus for longer periods of time and spot more mistakes, details or see angles that improve your work.

6. Use systems. While some people have stronger memory than others, all people have brains with limited capacity for recalling specific details. As you are brought into new matters, your workload will expand and your schedule will become more complicated. While you may be able to remember general details, the more specific ones will begin to get lost in the commotion. Common systems used by attorneys and interns alike are utilizing their Outlook or smartphone calendars, writing down "to-do lists" on a notepad or keeping a working document on the computer with a matrix of assignments, deadlines and other details.

7. Be organized. Writing down the important facts during a meeting is useless if you cannot locate those notes when you need them. Your workspace should operate as a finely-tuned machine. De-clutter your desk, stack papers and put them in folders and throw away or archive documents that you no longer need. Doing this will make you feel more focused and relaxed, which will sharpen your attention to detail.

8. Take breaks/get rest. It is important to take breaks from your work. This lets your mind rest and, when you return to your assignment, you will be better equipped to notice the details. Breaks do not need to be too long, a few minutes will do.

9. Stay calm. Anxiety and nervousness can severely disrupt focus. You should strive to perform your work in a relaxed mind state. This requires being self-aware. Pay close attention to your mood and anxiety level during your workday and practice stress management techniques to keep your attention to detail sharp.

Chapter 12

MANAGE YOUR STRESS

It may sound strange, but you want your internship to induce stress. If it does, that means that you are stretching yourself outside of your comfort zone and optimizing the benefits that a practical legal work experience has to offer. But at the same time, you shouldn't let the stress from these challenging situations impede your work performance or suppress your personality. You must learn to manage your stress.

The Negative Impacts of Stress

Managing stress begins with being able to identify that you are experiencing stress. Stress is the physical response to an event or circumstance that upsets your balance or normal routine. Your body's immediate stress response is increased heart rate and blood pressure, tightened muscles and quicker breath. This "fight or flight" mechanism is designed to help you avoid danger and can improve your work performance in the short-term. But, if left unmanaged for prolonged periods of time, stress can have a profound negative impact on:

- **Your mind:** memory problems, inability to concentrate and decreased focus, poor judgment, focusing on only the negative, anxiety, racing thoughts, fear, unease, worry or frustration.
- **Your body:** chest pain, rapid heartbeat, frequent colds, diarrhea, constipation, aches and pains.
- **Your mood:** Irritability, short temper, agitation and inability to relax, feeling overwhelmed, depressed or generally unhappy, lonely or isolated.
- **Your behavior:** decrease in appetite, loss of sleep or sleeping too much, withdrawing from relationships or socializing, procrastination or avoiding of responsibilities, nervous habits (biting nails, chewing cheek, twirling hair), using alcohol or drugs to unwind.

If you experience these negative effects of stress, you better believe that your work performance will suffer, along with your mind and body. This should be motivation enough to develop and practice identifying and managing stress. As detailed below, your internship will present many opportunities to do this.

Probable Stressors During Your Internship

Great achievement is never easy. You should expect and want your internship to present you with stressful situations. Here are a few common stressors for interns:

1. Relocation. If your internship is in a different locale, city or state, you may be living in a completely new residence with a new commute. Your living quarters, sleeping and waking up routine and commute may change drastically thereby causing stress.

> *Example Stressful Internship Situation:* *Your internship is in a new city. There are noises at night, and the garbage comes early in the morning both of which disrupt your sleep. You have to change the kind of coffee you drink in the morning and, to get to the office, you must cram yourself into an over-populated subway car that sporadically runs 15 minutes late.*
>
> ***Do you think that you'll be experiencing stress when you finally arrive at the office?***

2. Your workload. You may find yourself working harder than you ever had before during your internship. Juggling multiple assignments, prioritizing deadlines which may seem impossible to meet, working longer hours, getting into the office early in the morning, having to jump from assignment to assignment, shifting gears and creating work product in short, definitive time spans. You may also frequently get blindsided by receiving multiple assignments at once without any warning or ability to see it coming. It is also stress-inducing not being able to anticipate spikes in your workload, or knowing if you can keep personal plans outside of work, or keep a regular schedule.

> *Example Stressful Internship Situation:* *You arrive to work and on your to-do list is an internal memorandum of law due by 11:00am, a letter to opposing counsel by 1:30 pm, you have to deliver some documents to court at some point in the day, and you must fill out some administrative forms for the HR department. You sit at your desk, and there is a voicemail from your assigning attorney, and your computer isn't turning on.*
>
> ***Do you think that all of these overlapping assignments and a malfunctioning workspace will be frustrating?***

3. The people. The working style of your assigning attorneys may be hard to handle. They may speak in a condescending or harsh tone and only communicate to you criticism and no praise. They may be very anxious, which can be contagious and arouse your anxiety. They may make unreasonable demands like unrealistic deadlines or to be responsive over email at all times.

> *Example Stressful Internship Situation:* *Your assigning attorney emailed you last night at 10:00 pm directing you to make revisions to a letter that needs to be done by 8:00 am the following morning. You didn't see his email until 8:30 am the next morning during your commute into the office. When you arrive at your office, there's a note on your desk from him that says "see me." When you swing by his office, he has an angry look on his face and motions for you to take a seat while he finishes up a telephone call.*
>
> ***Do you think you will be nervous as you wait for this attorney to get off the telephone?***

4. The type of work. The assignments you are given may be completely new to you. New practice areas, new types of documents to create, new ways of presenting results, or new software to use. It will be stressful performing new tasks, making mistakes, receiving negative feedback, and grappling with a sometimes steep learning curve of developing new skills and abilities.

> *Example Stressful Internship Situation: Your assigning attorney asks you to write an Answer to a foreclosure Complaint in a state court lawsuit. He gives you the Complaint, some background information and general drafting tips. But you are still lost on how to do the assignment. You've never seen (let alone drafted) an Answer before, are not familiar with litigation in general or this particular state court procedure, and have no experience with foreclosures. The assigning attorney asks that you get her a draft by the end of the day and then leaves the office.*
>
> ***Do you think you may feel overwhelmed about how you're going to get the assignment done?***

5. High-Pressure Assignments. Attorneys are renowned for performing under some of the highest pressure situations that a workplace can provide. As an intern with little or no relevant exposure, you may have serious stress reactions to performing tasks in courtrooms, depositions, mediations, arbitrations, negotiations, investigations, hearings, client meetings or other events where every word is on the record or, at the least, highly-scrutinized.

> *Example Stressful Internship Situation: You help an attorney prepare for an oral argument in federal court. The day before, you compile and organize hundreds of pages of documents, including prior pleadings, deposition transcripts, exhibits, letters and legal research. The attorney tells you to be ready to provide him with any document in the file that he might need to argue the motion. You bring all of these documents with you to court and sit in the front pew. While the attorneys are waiting for the judge to enter the courtroom so oral argument can commence, the attorney looks back and asks you to give him a specific case. You now have to quickly sift through all the hundreds of pages and pull the case before the judge takes the bench and oral argument begins.*
>
> ***Do you think that your heart will be pounding as you try to locate the case with people watching, the attorney waiting and the judge about to enter the courtroom at any second?***

6. The work environment. Corporate culture or norms may vary greatly depending on the type of organization, industry, clientele, location, and/or practice area. Some people may be confrontational or passive aggressive, offices may be loud, competitive and fast pace. Others may be mellow and quiet, people may socialize frequently in and outside of the office or others may keep to themselves. A company's values, style of communication and overall "feel" of the workplace may take some adjustment.

> *Example Stressful Internship Situation: You get back to your desk after receiving a list of assignments, the first of which is to be completed within the hour. You crack your knuckles and settle into your chair to begin working when another attorney stops by your cubicle to make small talk. To be polite, you chat with her for fifteen minutes and then she leaves. When you look down at your computer, there is an email in your inbox from another*

attorney with an urgent tone telling you to come to his office immediately. After he gives you the assignment (which turns out to not be as urgent as initially indicated), the attorney makes small talk with you also. You feel the deadline for your first assignment rapidly approaching while you try to engage in the conversation. As a result of being polite and responding to an emergent email, you now may not meet your original deadline.

Do you think you'll have difficulty making polite small talk and listening while you keep getting distracted from getting your assignment done by the deadline?

7. The limited time. Most internships last for only a definitive period of time. This looming end date may create a sense of urgency for an intern to prove themselves, make a positive impression and potentially earn a position. It may seem like every minute, day, assignment or opportunity counts. It is stressful to work under such pressure and feeling like you don't have the luxury of easing into the position.

Example Stressful Internship Situation: You started your internship hoping to make a positive impression and potentially earn a post-graduate job offer in the real estate group, which is chaired by one partner. Early in the internship, you did an assignment for that partner who commented that you did an "ok" job. Many weeks passed without another assignment from that partner. Then, finally, with only two weeks left in your internship, you get another assignment from that partner. This may be your last opportunity to demonstrate your capabilities, develop a relationship and impress her. The assignment is very difficult with a tight deadline.

Do you think you'll feel like all of your job prospects are riding on this one, last, difficult assignment?

8. Personal Life. The pressures and demands between work and personal life often become blurred. While you are pushing yourself to adapt to and overcome the challenges during your internship, you may also be simultaneously navigating complicated, emotionally-charged and highly important personal issues involving your family, friends, loved ones and you. Dealing with these personal issues outside of the office then being able to compartmentalize them in order to focus on your work is much easier said than done. But every successful professional must learn how to do this.

Example Stressful Internship Situation: You wake up to a telephone call from your sibling that your parent, who lives across the country, is sick in a hospital. There is nothing you can do and you can't fly home until the doctors learn more about your parent's condition. Your sibling tells you that they will call you back in the afternoon with an update. You then get ready and go to the office for a very important meeting.

Do you think that you will be stressed out and have difficulty concentrating during that meeting?

Stress Management Techniques

Once you are able to observe your stress reactions to these situations, there are a number of different stress management techniques available to neutralize your stress. Some techniques are designed to respond to stress that arises quickly and in the moment. Other stress management techniques are intended for coping with stressors that exist in the work environment generally.

On-the-Spot Stress Management

1. Be present. When your mind becomes cluttered and prevents you from thinking straight and performing your work, re-calibrate your mind state. Slow down and stop doing anything for a moment. Take an overview of your current situation. Focus on your breathing until you feel your heart rate calming down and your mind starts to clear.

2. Get organized. Sometimes your workload can seem like an insurmountable challenge. In these moments, break it down into pieces and tackle one assignment at a time. Map out your assignments, make to do lists, charts, with deadlines and details. Visualizing your plan of attacking your workload will help relieve the stress and get started.

3. Self-reassurance. In moments when you are feeling overwhelmed, it helps to redirect your thoughts to what is important and real. Reaffirm yourself that you are smart, capable, prepared, and the organization hired you because they believe you can get the job done. Convincing yourself to be confident will help clear the cobwebs and get to work.

4. Prepare. A great way to reduce your stress about an upcoming event, assignment or situation is to prepare as much as possible. Anticipate tasks, issues, problems, questions or documents that may be involved, and ensure that you are ready to respond in the moment.

5. Embrace what you cannot change. This is an eternal and universal truth that must be applied to your internship. There will be many stressors that are out of your control. It is illogical to waste your time and energy worrying about these things that you cannot change. Simply accept them and move forward. Focus your energy on outcomes that you can impact.

6. Try not to worry. Sometimes the biggest sources of stress can be thoughts of what may happen if you fail. What if I can't find the case? What if I forget the client's name? The answer should always be: "It will be fine." Because it will. Nothing is the end of the world. All you can do is work hard, prepare, and do your best.

7. Reach out. If you are in need of advice, guidance, insight or general assistance that is otherwise unattainable on your own, reach out to co-workers or colleagues and bring them into your situation. The most experienced practitioners will tell you that sometimes it makes more sense to ask a colleague a question rather than needlessly laboring over a task for hours.

8. Find humor. Never take yourself too seriously. Laughter makes us feel good. Inserting levity into a tense situation can loosen your mood, lower your stress level, and enable you to think more clearly.

General Lifestyle Stress Management

1. Sleep and eat well. These two aspects of everyday life often get lost in the shuffle when work schedules get hectic. Don't let this happen. Prioritize getting at least 7 or 8 hours of sleep each night and eating a balanced diet. Your cognitive functioning, mood and ability to react to stress depend on it.

2. Exercise. Attorneys (and interns) tend to spend their days in a sedentary state, sitting in chairs. Try to go for at least a walk every day. If your schedule permits, go for a bicycle ride, run, swim, do cardio exercises, weightlift or play sports. It is undeniable that physical activity reduces stress, lifts spirits, and increases mental functioning.

3. Maintain healthy relationships. Do not to permit a heavy workload to push you into an isolated lifestyle. Even though it takes effort and time, it is important to socialize with your co-workers and stay connected with friends, loved ones and family. Maintaining a sense of community and relying on a strong support system helps to decompress and overcome a stressful work environment.

4. Relaxation. To balance out all of the time you spend being productive (working, sleeping, exercising, etc.), you should do things that bring you tranquility. Practice yoga, meditation or tai chi. Get massages, watch television or movies, or read for leisure. These relaxing experiences will help you stay centered, balanced, and ready to respond positively to stressful situations.

5. Avoid bad habits. The shortsighted way to respond to stress is through bad habits, such as drinking, smoking, over or under eating, withdrawing from friends and family, procrastinating, engaging in repetitive non-productive negative thinking cycles or taking out your stress on others through rude behavior or outbursts. If you feel compelled to engage in some of these bad habits, *without judging yourself*, make a pivot and instead practice the good habits described above.

> Side Note: There are many different types of professionals that can be instrumental in dealing with stress on the spot and also in implementing positive stress management habits in our everyday life. Executive coaches, psychologists, career counselors, or attorney help-lines are all resources that are available to you when encountering stressful situations. You can find these professionals online on your own, or reach out to your law school career counselors who can steer you in the right direction.

Chapter 13

UPWARDLY MANAGE YOUR ASSIGNING ATTORNEYS

When trying to work well with assigning attorneys, many interns simply follow one rule — do whatever I am told to do. While that is certainly important, it is not enough. To stand out, you must be a dynamic and forward-thinking employee and sensitive to your assigning attorneys' needs — even if they do not verbalize those needs. You must be adept at upward management.

Upward management is the process of aligning yourself with your assigning attorney in a way that promotes efficiency, clarity of expectations, trust, quality work product, and an overall enjoyable working relationship. It is a skill that must be learned on the job and tailored to each attorney. If you excel at it, you may become so embedded into your assigning attorney(s)'s practice that they come to think of you as indispensable. This is what you want.

Follow Direction

If you are fortunate enough to have an assigning attorney who has the time, patience and awareness to give you clear directions on your work performance, follow these directions without fail. This tenet of upward management is paramount; nothing else matters if you cannot follow instructions. This goes for general and specific instructions.

Some examples of the types of **<u>general instructions</u>** you may receive from assigning attorneys include:

- <u>When to arrive/leave the office</u> — One of an intern's greatest assets is the ability to be "Johnny-on-the-spot" and be around the office when an extra hand is needed. If you are expected to be at the office for certain hours, be there.
- <u>Your physical appearance</u> — How you dress and maintain your physical appearance is a reflection on how you approach your work. Your assigning attorney(s) look at you on a daily basis. If they make comments or give direct feedback about how you should dress/shave, etc., follow their direction.
- <u>Their preferred manner of communication</u> — Some attorneys prefer most communications to be done over email. Others prefer in-person meetings or for you to call them. Some prefer if you constantly check in with them and others may tell you not to bombard them and wait for them to contact you. If your assigning attorney(s) tells you what manner of communication they prefer, follow this instruction.

- Presenting or performing assignments — The general instructions an attorney might give about how they want work performed can vary greatly, such as always printing/highlighting case law cited in a memo, saving documents or organizing files in a certain way, using certain terminology. Follow these instructions when applicable.

Whatever general instructions you may receive from assigning attorneys that relates to your overall performance of work during your internship, be sure to take seriously and follow. These are the roadmap to meeting their expectations.

Overlaying these general instructions will be the **specific instructions** that you receive pertaining to how to perform an individual assignment, such as:

- The deadline — Do they want a status update at the end of the day, first draft or final draft? Should you check in at some point?
- The work product format — Do they want an email, formal memo, chart, table or final draft of a contract? What information must be included? What is the structure?
- The manner of communicating the results — Do they want you to call, email, save on the system, or meet in person to discuss and bring notes? Do they want back-up data, documents or case law included?
- Method of performance — Did they specify how they wanted you to perform the work? Review certain print or electronic resources, talk to someone, or work off of a particular document?

Keep in mind that most attorneys are usually quite particular about what they want done and how they want it done. Sometimes they explain the reasoning behind their specifications to you. Other times they are simply too busy or short on patience to go through it with you. Regardless of how the instructions are communicated, do not discount them.

Listen actively and ask questions to understand exactly what they want. Of course, always ask for clarification if a specific instruction conflicts with a general instruction they've already given. Otherwise, write down the instructions and do as they say. Nothing is more displeasing to an attorney than having their carefully constructed and communicated instructions disregarded.

Know Your Assigning Attorney

Relatively speaking, it is easy to follow direction. But not all attorneys are great communicators at how they want work performed. Some are simply so busy they struggle to get all of their own work done; so they do not have the bandwidth to tell you how you should be doing your work.

To separate yourself from other interns who simply follow direction and nothing else, get to know your assigning attorney and anticipate their needs. This requires stepping outside yourself, observing your assigning attorney's work environment, communication style, preferences, pressures, values, and working style. Then, based on what you observe, think about what they may need or prefer from you and provide it. This is the hallmark of upward management.

A good way to start this analysis is by considering what your assigning attorney values the most. The following table represents the four "DISC" profile factors. Based on what they do and say, try to deduce where in the table your assigning attorney's values are:

Dominance. *Are they bottom-line driven and only care about the results? Are they blunt, outwardly confident, get straight to the point and focus on the big picture?*	**Influential.** *Do they place emphasis on personal interaction, connections and relationships? Are they enthusiastic, collaborative and optimistic?*
Steadiness. *Do they communicate that consistency, dependability, sincerity and steadiness are important traits to them? Do they not like being rushed and work in a calm manner?*	**Conscientiousness.** *Are they constantly encouraging conscientiousness? Do they care very much about quality, accuracy, expertise and competency? Do they like working independently or engaging in objective reasoning?*

By understanding what your assigning attorney values the most, you can then modify your conduct to align with their values. This is not a suggestion that you change who you are. Rather, that you emphasize and elevate certain aspects of your personality and working style to make your combined effort more productive and relationship stronger.

Consider the following suggestions on how to align with your assigning attorney's values and working style:

- If they are "**Dominance**" — make sure you are constantly reinforcing to them your willingness to get the job done, no matter what it takes.
- If they are "**Influential**" — appeal to their relational values. Let them know you appreciate their mentorship and the positive effects it will have on your overall career. Ask them for advice when appropriate.
- If they are "**Steadiness**" — above all else, be consistent. Don't be late, don't forget things, set reminders, plan ahead, make sure you always have plenty of time to perform your work and don't say anything confidently unless you are certain it is true.
- If they are "**Conscientiousness**" — sweat the details. Review their work and catch typos and grammatical errors. Make sure everything you create is perfectly organized, complete, accurate and a "final" version.

Keep a lookout for indicators that your assigning attorney falls into one of those categories so you can anticipate their expectations and act in a way designed to meet those expectations.

Another factor to consider is the incentives which apply to your assigning attorney. What are they trying to accomplish on a daily basis? Who do they report to? Are they trying to satisfy a particular client or appeal to a supervising partner? If it is a government organization, are there political pressures involved? Try to figure out what motivates them. This will help you understand the big picture from their perspective and make you more capable of working in a way that aligns with their needs.

Anticipate and Align Your Work with Their Needs

Your assigning attorneys have their own work style. They have their own schedule (or lack thereof), work environment, clientele, preferences, demands and manner in which they get their work done. Observe these conditions and "upward manage" your assigning attorneys by fitting your working style into theirs.

Here are a few common types of general work styles that you may encounter during your internship and suggestions on how to align yourself:

1. **The assigning attorney travels frequently and has difficulty getting in front of a computer throughout the day.**

- Send documents in a format that can be opened and viewed on a smart phone.
- Be available for telephone calls at times that align with their meeting schedules.
- Send them a quick email when you're stepping out of the office throughout the day and won't be able to answer your work phone.
- Be responsive to email early and late in the day when they are able to sit down at their computer and respond to emails.

2. **The assigning attorney has an enormous workload and tends to forget details.**

- Don't take it personally when they are non-responsive to your emails.
- Send them reminders to make sure things don't slip through the cracks.
- Offer to take care of smaller tasks that they apparently cannot get to.
- Always bring extra copies of documents for them regardless if they've already been provided with them.

> Side Note: Attorneys with enormous workloads tend to delegate a lot. Working for these attorneys will invariably present many opportunities to gain experience in advanced, higher-level tasks. Increased responsibility means increased rewards. When they delegate, be sure to acknowledge receipt, confirm you are "on it," and be sure to get the work done right. There will be plenty more where that came from.

3. **The assigning attorney tends to wait until the last minute to get things done.**

- Emphasize urgency when you remind them that a deadline is approaching.

- Anticipate details or third party involvement that must be coordinated in order to get work done on time.
- Clear your schedule for a few hours before a deadline so you are ready and available to help get the work finished on time.
- Advise ahead of time if you have a conflict that might prevent you from being available in the final hours leading up to a deadline.

In addition, your assigning attorney may display certain individual preferences that you need to pick up on in order to align with their working and communication style. For instance:

• ***Your assigning attorney may work in a scattered, multi-tasking manner throughout the day.*** Their workday may constantly bounce back and forth between tasks, answering calls and emails, in-person conversations, or engaging in dialogues with people popping into their office. If so, be sure to assertively interrupt their workflow to engage them on matters where you need their assistance or input.

• ***Your assigning attorney may work in a focused, singular manner.*** They may schedule meetings in lieu of impromptu discussions and calls, let unanticipated calls go to voicemail, and only respond to emails during certain periods of the day. If so, you should learn to work in this focused manner and abide by their scheduling requirements in order to meet with them. This may take more discipline, preparation and forethought where each meeting has a designated purpose.

• ***Your assigning attorney may be protective over their client relationships.*** If so, always double-check that it is acceptable for you to communicate directly with their client and be sensitive to each and every "touch point" where a client is contacted.

• ***Your assigning attorney may arrive at the office early.*** If so, you should shift your work schedule to be available for work early in the day as well, be particularly vigilant in checking emails in early hours and advise if you are running late.

• ***Your assigning attorney may prefer to stay in constant contact over email.*** If so, you should become accustomed to responding to email throughout the day and even outside of business hours. Get in the habit of checking your emails and responding quickly (but always thoughtfully).

• ***Your assigning attorney may enjoy small talk and getting to know you on a personal level.*** If so, you should make sure you are comfortable with and tactful about the personal information you share. There is nothing wrong with opening up, so long as it does not jeopardize your professional image.

• ***Your assigning attorney may prefer meeting in person.*** If so, make a habit of swinging by their office, "pop in" to check in with them and gauge how they react to that. If they seem annoyed, stop doing it.

> Side Note: It is not unheard of to ask your assigning attorney directly what they prefer. If they are sending you mixed signals (telling you to swing by

their office but acting annoyed when you arrive, telling you to send them emails then not responding, etc.) just ask them directly: "Do you prefer it if I . . . ." Listen to the answer then act according to whatever they tell you.

You want to be the piece that fits perfectly into your assigning attorney's workday. Keep in mind what they need and be it.

Dos and Don'ts of Upwardly Managing Your Assigning Attorney

Keeping in mind that your working style should be tailored to each individual assigning attorney, there are some general "dos" and "don'ts" of upward management that should be followed during your internship:

- DO: **Provide objective facts, not opinions.** Interns are frequently the least experienced person in the room. This means that they are invited to contribute in a narrow way - observe, listen, learn and, if asked, provide facts. Don't cloud those facts with your emotions or subjective interpretations. Let the attorneys receive those facts and interpret them in accordance with the bigger picture to make their subjective determination on how to proceed. That is their job, not yours.

- DON'T: **Say only what they want to hear.** Your assigning attorney may be delegating work to you and expecting you to get it done. That does not mean that it will always get done in the way they expect. Don't hide important facts or circumstances that they may not be pleased with. They need to know everything that is material. If you withhold information and they find out later, they will lose trust in you.

- DO: **Respect the assigning attorney's time.** Always be sensitive to the opportunity cost for an attorney's expenditure of time with you. Every minute they are training you, giving you assignments, and sharing feedback on your work product is time away from the pile of work on their desk or with their family and friends. No matter how terse or distracted they may seem, they are investing their time in you which comes at a high cost for them. Whenever possible, demonstrate that that you appreciate and respect their time. If you have a meeting, create an agenda beforehand, have your notes prepared and organized, be ready for questions, listen attentively and thank them for their time when appropriate.

- DON'T: **Leave the assigning attorney in the dark.** When given an assignment, don't conceal information to prove to them that you can get things done on your own. You want to be autonomous. But they need progress reports from you. A quick email or call letting them know you finished an assignment can jostle their memory and spark the next step or a new assignment. Falling off the grid completely will only bring them anxiety and frustration that they were kept in the dark. Be sure to periodically check in/make yourself visible to your assigning attorney.

- DO: **Always preserve your credibility.** Relationships, especially working relationships between legal professionals, are built on trust. Always make sure you follow through on your commitments, avoid saying things with confidence that later turn out to be untrue, quickly writing an email that contains mistakes or misstatements, showing up late or missing meetings, forgetting important events, misplacing documents, submitting incomplete work product or appearing overly emotional with your work. These types of missteps can erode credibility and make your co-workers inwardly or outwardly question your words. You never want this to happen.

- DON'T: **Over-share.** Don't share every single detail with your assigning attorney about an assignment and force them to comb through what you are saying to figure out what is important. This wastes time and energy and may cause them to lose interest in hearing what you have to say. It also reflects that you might not understand what is important. Distill down in your head the highlights and give them only that. The attorney can always ask questions to fill in any holes. Plus, their questions will be instructive to you on what they find important.

- DO: **Make your assigning attorney look good.** Be your assigning attorney's right hand. Make them look good. This will be good for you also. Put your assigning attorney in a position to succeed and impress their clients, colleagues or superiors. Provide them with critical information before a court appearance or presentation, catch typos in their work product and remind them of important tasks or events. Do all that you can to make sure that they get it done correctly.

Chapter 14

NAIL THE LEGAL RESEARCH ASSIGNMENT

At the most basic level, your legal internship experience is comprised of a series of work assignments. Each assignment presents an opportunity to shape the organization's perception of your capabilities. It is your time to demonstrate strong performance, prove your worth and convince the organization that it can accomplish more with you on the team. Regardless of the actual assignment, this should always be your goal.

There are myriad assignments that you might be given during your internship. While some assignments are typical in a particular practice area — such as due diligence review in corporate law or organizing exhibits for litigation matters — it is virtually impossible to accurately predict what your assignments will be during your internship. Thus, to a large extent, you must simply be ready to perform.

However, you can be certain that, at some point during your internship, you will be given a legal research assignment that involves conducting legal research and presenting the results in writing, verbally, or both.

This chapter walks through the different steps of a legal research assignment. At each, there is general guidance and specific tips for avoiding common mistakes, overcoming challenges, working efficiently, and generally how to perform well.

Receiving the Assignment

The most important moment in a legal research assignment is the exchange through which you receive an assignment from the attorney. This is your first and best opportunity to acquire all of the necessary information to formulate your research strategy, assure that your work product is delivered on time and answers the question asked in the right tone and format.

Here are a few pointers to keep in mind during the assignment intake:

A. Focus on every word. Avoid letting a busy environment, fast-talking attorney or your own stress level prevent you from focusing intently on what the assigning attorney tells you.

B. Ask clarity questions. If something the assigning attorney says is ambiguous, unclear, unintelligible or incomplete, be sure to ask questions in the moment to ensure you understand everything they say. Trust your gut. If you were focusing on every word, then there's probably a good reason why you didn't understand something they said.

C. Ask big picture questions. Try to obtain a reasonable amount of relevant background details, such as the end-user(s) of your work product, the industry, client(s), factual and procedural history.

D. Ask strategy questions. Any wisdom an assigning attorney can share regarding "how they would handle" the task or their "hunch" regarding the results can be enormously helpful in formulating your research strategy.

E. Ask practical questions. Don't let the attorney leave without informing you when the assignment is due, how they want the results presented (i.e., memo, email, swing by office to talk, print/highlight/tab cases, etc.) or any other important information such as client or matter number for internal filing purposes, any other attorneys involved or contact information.

F. Don't ask "stupid" questions. There is such a thing as a stupid question during a legal internship. Unless it is critical for you to understand the rest of the assignment, don't ask the attorney a question that can be answered through a Google search.

G. Write down as much as possible. Your memory cannot be trusted. Your notes will be your security blanket when the assigning attorney is gone and you need to remember key phrases, specific facts, the purpose or other critical details of the assignment. If you have questions but don't want to interrupt, write those down also and ask when the assigning attorney finishes their thought. Don't worry about your penmanship.

H. Communicate your situation. If your current workload or work schedule (upcoming vacation/personal day) makes it unrealistic that you can meet the assigned deadline, convey that information assertively and respectfully to the assigning attorney. If possible, offer a potential resolution or alternative. But always try to meet/beat the deadline if possible.

> *Assignment Case Study:* *An attorney calls you to their office to give you an assignment. She is visibly rushed and distracted. She says "I just need some quick case law research. I need to know whether we should bring a motion to dismiss an individual plaintiff's discrimination lawsuit filed in 2010 in federal court because she received a discharge in bankruptcy court but failed to disclose the claims on a personal bankruptcy petition she filed in 2011. If you could, I would love the answer by the end of the day. Thanks." Then the attorney turns back to their desk and continues writing an email.*

Don't let this be the end of the conversation. The assigning attorney may not realize that you need more information in order to get started. Try to gauge her tone and answers to make the most of the intake interaction.

Try asking follow up questions:

- *You ask: "What kind of discrimination claim is it?" She responds "housing discrimination."*
- *You ask: "In what federal court is the case pending?" She responds: "Eastern District of New York."*
- *You ask: "What bankruptcy court was her case filed in?" She responds: "Also EDNY."*

- *You ask: "Sorry to make you repeat this, but I'm a little confused. You said she filed her discrimination lawsuit in 2010 and that the lawsuit was filed after her bankruptcy discharge in 2011? That doesn't seem to add up." She responds: "Sorry, good catch. I meant to say that the discrimination lawsuit was filed in 2014."*
- *You ask: "Do you have any guess or hunch as to why the discrimination case might be subject to dismissal?" She responds: "I think, but am not sure, that something like judicial estoppel might apply. But I really don't know. That's why I need your help."*
- *You ask: "Do you have a suggested research strategy?" She says: "I really don't, sorry. You can figure it out. Anything else?" You sense she's starting to rush you to finish the conversation.*
- *You ask: "Last question — how should I present my results and when do you want it?" She responds: "Please write me an email and attach the cases. By the end of today is fine."*
- *You ask: "Attorney Richardson had asked me to assist him with a deposition this afternoon that will probably end around 5:30pm. I don't think I would be able to start the research until after. Should I tell him that I cannot attend?" She responds: "No, that's ok. By the end of the day tomorrow is fine."*

No assignment intake process is the same. Some attorneys may be terse, impatient and unclear. Others may be chatty, enjoy explaining the background and answering questions. These personal interactions will vary enormously depending on the organization, the attorney, the particular day, case or assignment. But if you can stick to these guidelines, you'll have the best chance to start your assignment on the right foot.

> Side Note: You may receive assignments via email also. Be sure to follow the same assignment intake guidelines over email to ensure that you exchange all the necessary information with the assigning attorney.

Formulating Your Legal Research Strategy

The tendency for most law students is to jump right into the research with little forethought. Such urgency may be caused by mounting deadlines, shrinking time-frames, an eagerness to get started or a comment from the assigning attorney that it is a "quick assignment." Regardless, be patient and calculated. Take a moment to plan out your strategy before launching into action.

A. Sit Back and Think. Sometimes the hardest thing to do during a busy day is nothing. But this is what you must do before any legal research assignment. Sit back in your chair, go for a walk and calmly think through all of the issues ahead. Try to analyze the problem from multiple angles and assess different strategies for finding the answer.

B. Reread the Question. Make sure you understand the background, relevant issues and purpose of the assignment and what really matters. You must know exactly what the problem is if you are going to solve it.

C. Formulate Research Strategy. Assess what you know, what you need to know and what resources are available to you to bridge the gap. If you already possess a wealth of experience in the subject matter of the assignment, then you may want to employ a targeted strategy that leads you directly to the answer. If you are in unfamiliar territory (new practice area, jurisdiction, industry, etc.), consider spending the time gaining background information so you can understand the big picture.

> *Assignment Case Study (cont'd): You have many questions. You have no academic or practical experience in bankruptcy, discrimination law, or federal litigation. Thus, your research strategy should begin with a meaningful exploration into this new universe by learning the applicable laws/regulations and the purposes behind them, the relevant tribunals and interplay between them, the key words and terminology and anything else that would get you up to speed with the subject matter. Only after you gain this background information will you be able to efficiently navigate your way to the case law.*

D. Consider Time Constraints. In a perfect world, you would have unlimited time to search all ends of the earth for information to help you answer the research question. But, in reality, you will likely have some deadline for presenting your results. Factor in time constraints when deciding how to allocate your time during your research assignment to make sure you don't run out of time. Sometimes, especially in a busy law office, attorneys are simply doing the best they can with the time and resources given. You will be expected to do the same.

E. Consider Your Assigning Attorney. This ties into your upward management skills. Think about your assigning attorney's preferences when mapping out your strategy on how to conduct the research and present the results. Will they be highly critical of your writing? If so, make sure you don't get too bogged down in researching and allocate enough time to the writing and proofreading phase. Will they likely fire many questions at you about your legal research strategy? If so, then make sure you keep track of each step of your legal research. Anticipate their needs and keep them in mind when constructing your strategy.

F. Use Your Calendar. Be cognizant of how much time you have and calendar all important deadlines. This assignment may be the most important thing in your world when the intake is over. But, one minute later, another attorney may come around the corner and give you a new, more pressing assignment. If that happens, your focus will shift, and the current assignment will fade into the background. But it remains just as important, so be sure to calendar when the assignment is due and set reminders. Sometimes double calendaring is a good method — outlook calendar and paper.

> Side Note: If you are in such unfamiliar territory that your ability to meet the assigned deadline is questionable, you may want to consider returning to the

assigning attorney and letting them know.

Conducting Legal Research

Research is a fundamental component of practicing law. Every decision made by an attorney on behalf of a client should be supported, in some way and on some level, by controlling, up-to-date law. Thus, a lawyer (and legal intern) will always be judged based on their ability to efficiently locate, correctly interpret and apply the law.

As expected, every research assignment is different and necessitates a unique strategy. Here are some pointers on conducting legal research during your internship:

1. **Start with Google.** Google and other online search tools have become an increasingly powerful research and problem-solving tool — especially when practicing law. Intelligent use of Google can quickly (and without any cost) bring you to various websites containing free legal updates, articles, journals, commentary or other reliable secondary resources that may even contain citations to primary sources. Virtually every government agency maintains a website with applicable secondary and primary sources such as state and federal statutes, regulations, opinion letters, guides, handbooks, forms, manuals, updates and legislative records (bills, amendments, transcripts, etc.).

Assignment Case Study (cont'd): If your research strategy involves gaining background information to learn the applicable laws, tribunals, procedures, terminology and key words, then start with Google:

1. Google: "federal dismiss statute pleadings" *— takes you to www.law.cornell.edu that shows statutory text of Fed. R. Civ. P. 12(b) listing the 7 grounds to assert a defense to a pleading in federal court, one of which is "failure to state a claim under which relief may be granted" (Rule 12(b)(6)).*

2. Google: "federal housing discrimination claims" *— takes you to https:blogs.law.harvard.edu. Shows case updates on recent housing discrimination cases involving Federal Housing Act, 42 U.S.C. Section 3601, and the Civil Rights Act of 1866, 42 U.S.C. Sections 1981–1982.*

3. Google: "FHA claims" *— takes you to www.abajournal.com. Shows you an article about how the US Supreme Court may opine on a housing discrimination claim.*

4. Google: "42 U.S.C. Section 1981 claim" *— takes you to www.federalevidence.com. Shows you a treatise about how to bring a race discrimination claim.*

5. Google: "Bankruptcy Petition provision" *— takes you to www.irs.gov. Shows you a "Legal Reference Guide for Revenue Officers" which lays out the "General Provisions of Bankruptcy." Click on section 5.17.8.6 entitled "Voluntary and Involuntary Bankruptcies." This now gives an explanation of how a bankruptcy is instituted through the filing of a petition with citation to specific statutory provisions.*

> ***6. Google: "Bankruptcy discharge meaning"*** *— takes you to www.uscourts.gov. Shows you a FAQ page with all sorts of information on what, when, where and why how a bankruptcy discharge happens, including information on the involvement of a U.S. Trustee, the different chapters in bankruptcy and the types of debt dischargeable under the Bankruptcy Code.*
>
> ***7. Google: "judicial estoppel doctrine"*** *— takes you to law firm's "Litigation Alert" newsletter with an article on judicial estoppel from 2010. The article explains that judicial estoppel is an equitable doctrine that bars a party from taking inconsistent positions in different proceedings and is applied by judges in order to preserve the court's integrity. It also cites a state court case in Westchester, NY entitled Matter of Hartsdale Fire District v. Eastland, in June 2010.*
>
> ***8. Google: "Hartsdale Fire District Eastland June 2010 Westchester"*** *— takes you to www.findlaw.com where you can read the text of the judicial estoppel case.*

Once you gain enough background information, you will have some key words and references to primary sources to formulate your research strategy on your favorite legal research databases, like Lexis Nexis.

2. Find controlling primary sources. Armed with what you've learned on free websites, now use your legal research database (i.e., Lexis Nexis) to find the cases, statutes/regulations and administrative decisions needed to solve your problem and confirm they are all "good law." Generally speaking, Google searches should supplement, but never replace, using a legal research database.

3. Narrow your search. The most common research strategy on legal databases is a key word search. If this strategy makes sense for your assignment, you should begin your search of the database by preliminarily assessing how many cases/statutes involve your particular legal issue. This can be done by starting with the most popular key words and narrowing your search from there until you yield a reasonable number of results where it makes sense to start reading in-depth:

> *<u>Assignment Case Study (cont'd):</u> You are unsure whether your particular subject matter and situation is extremely common or rare. So you start with some key word searches and narrow from there:*
>
> - *Search all federal cases containing the words: "bankruptcy" "dismiss" "discrimination" — yields 1,160 cases.*
> - *Search only Second Circuit federal cases containing the words: "bankruptcy" "dismiss" "discrimination" — yields 150 cases.*
> - *Search Second Circuit federal cases containing the words "bankruptcy" dismiss" discrimination" and "judicial estoppel" — yields 78 cases.*

> Side Note: Make sure you familiarize yourself with the cost structure of the internship organization's legal research tool. For example, you should understand whether the organization is charged per each search or according to the time spent. This should factor into your research strategy.

4. Efficiently review search results. Once you narrow down the search to a reasonable number of cases within your jurisdiction each containing a relevant arrangement of your search terms, start reading the cases. But don't read for pleasure. Read for utility. Now that you're "plugged in" to the community of decisions addressing the subject matter, efficiently review the cases with an eye towards spotting the same procedural posture, similar fact patterns and/or relevant legal analyses. A case containing one or more of these elements is "on point."

If your review does not yield any on-point cases, go back and modify your search terms. If you find an on-point case, read further to assess its application and use it to find additional on-point cases and/or statutes.

Keep in mind that, as you continue to dig deeper into the case law, new issues and questions may arise. Make note of these questions and seek guidance from the assigning attorney when appropriate.

> *Assignment Case Study (cont'd): Once you have narrowed down the cases to 78, you start reading. You begin reading only cases in the Eastern District that were decided in the last five years. Eventually, you find a case that deals with a relevant fact pattern, called Ayazi v. New York City Bd. of Educ., decided by the Second Circuit Court of Appeals in 2009. You read that case and the lower court decisions that it affirmed/modified. The issues are very similar and the holding is not favorable to your position — namely, it does not support dismissal. But there are some facts in Ayazi that you are not sure exist here. First, the plaintiff in Ayazi was pro se. Second, the plaintiff in Ayazi had her estate "abandoned" by the bankruptcy court, which is apparently a term of art under the Bankruptcy Code.*
>
> *You do some ancillary research to learn about "abandonment" within the bankruptcy context. Once that is done, you go back to your assigning attorney and ask some follow up questions:*
>
> *You ask: "Is our plaintiff pro se? Because I've found some case that appears on point, but that plaintiff is pro se." She responds: "No, she was represented by an attorney in her bankruptcy."*
>
> *You ask: "Do you know if her estate was abandoned by the trustee in bankruptcy court?" She responds: "I don't know. We don't have access to those papers right now."*

5. Navigate the relevant law. Once you do find an on-point case, there are usually other useful resources nearby. If your research assignment requires a comprehensive review of the case law (which it usually does), use your on-point cases to locate more. Bounce around the family of cases that touch on the relevant subject matter. This is how you fully research an issue. There is no single method to uncovering every applicable primary resource. Every situation is different. But here are three common research strategies for navigating the law:

A. ***Shepardize Forward.*** Explore the cases that cite your on-point case. Read those cases *and the cases that cite them*. Continue to go down each line of cases to find more on-point cases. If you reach an off-point case, go back to the last on-point case and start down another line of cases. Continue in this process until you exhaustively read every on-point case. Confronting the same cases over and over again is an indication that this has happened.

Assignment Case Study (cont'd): You Shepardize the Ayazi case and learn that it was cited by 18 other cases, one of which is a case entitled Ibok v. Siac-Sector Inc., a SDNY decision in 2011. Ibok (and its affirmance by the Second Circuit) reached a decision favorable to your position. You put Ibok aside for deeper analysis. Then you Shepardize Ibok. This yields 5 cases, one of which is entitled Amash v. Home Depot U.S.A., Inc., a NDNY case decided in 2013 that also reaches a favorable holding. Amash only cites Ayazi and Ibok, so you hit the end of this line. So you go back and read the other 4 cases that cite Ibok. None of them contain relevant case law. You go back further to the 18 cases that cite Ayazi and start reading the rest of those. You continue in this process until you've uncovered the entire family of cases that address this issue. You put these cases aside for further analysis.

B. ***Shepardize Backward.*** Check the cases upon which your on-point case relies. Read them thoroughly and *read the cases that they cite*. Exploring the case law backwards will introduce the earlier case law that developed the applicable legal principles and potentially open new lines of cases that you can then Shepardize forward. Continue this process of working backward and forward until you hit the end of the each line of cases. Keep track of the search history to ensure you went down each path.

Assignment Case Study (cont'd): The analysis in the Ayazi case that deals with whether to dismiss the discrimination claim cites two cases from the Second Circuit. You read these cases and learn that they do not deal with discrimination or bankruptcy. It appears that the Ayazi court was the first court in the Second Circuit to address and decide this issue. You feel comfortable that you do not need to go back any further.

C. ***Explore relevant statutes and regulations.*** There may be some statutory provisions or regulations that are a common thread in all relevant cases. Be sure to Shepardize the cases that cite these statutes/regulations.

Assignment Case Study (cont'd): Through the research, you learn that the abandonment of a debtor's estate can only be done pursuant to Section 554 of the Bankruptcy Code. So you Shepardize and run a search of all Second Circuit cases that cite this provision of the Code, along with key words "judicial estoppel." This yields 11 additional cases that are on-point. You read these cases and find two other cases that deal with abandonment and judicial estoppel. One is the Ibok case. The other is a case with very different fact pattern.

Now that you are frequently encountering the same cases, you conclude that you have reviewed every Second Circuit decision that deals with these issues and are ready to synthesize the information and render your legal opinion.

6. Consider negative treatment. Don't forget this critical step of research. If Shepardizing uncovers that an on-point case has negative treatment, read and assess whether the negative treatment impacts the precedential value of the case. Your case may have had subsequent treatment that erodes part of its holding or completely prevents it from being "good law." Or, it could be that it was remanded, modified, or overturned on unrelated legal issues leaving your analysis unaffected. Either way, you need to know and be able to address any subsequent treatment of your cases.

7. Keep track of on-point cases. As you bounce from case to case immersed in your legal research, you will be absorbing and assimilating information. It may not be readily apparent which aspects of those cases will be useful throughout the assignment. So keep track of the cases as you move forward. Use whatever system works for you to go back and efficiently locate the cases that you need.

8. Reach out to a junior attorney. If you are comfortable and they are approachable, consider asking another attorney for suggestions on how to navigate your research. They may be more than happy to help.

9. Call for help. Legal research databases typically have specialists available to provide assistance in your legal research efforts. As a last resort, call them and seek guidance. Just be sure that you not only get their advice, but you use the experience to help improve your own legal research skills. Pay attention to how they approach the assignment and where you may have went wrong.

> Side Note: Legal research can be a highly anxiety-provoking task. The research may be difficult, complex, or nuanced. You may not have enough information. Or, as is most common, you may be given a long-shot "see if you can find a case that says . . . " research assignment. Make sure that you don't let your anxiety get the best of you, as this can seriously disrupt concentration and reading comprehension. If you are feeling overwhelmed, try changing research strategies, seeking guidance from a trusted mentor, or some stress management techniques described above.

Once you've finished conducting legal research, applying the applicable legal principles to the underlying facts and reaching your conclusions, it is time to communicate your findings to the assigning attorney — in writing and/or verbally.

These communications during your internship are highly-influential of your success. In other words, your efficiency, clarity, and tone while communicating the results of your legal research can largely shape an organization's perception of you. For that reason, each occasion to write for and speak with an assigning attorney about your legal research results should be approached with the utmost diligence.

Writing Out the Results of Your Legal Research

Writing assignments can take many forms during an internship. At the most formal end of the spectrum, you may be asked to write a memorandum for submission to a client or judge. A less formal writing assignment may be a legal analysis to be inserted into a larger memorandum, an internal memorandum drafted for the file or to familiarize an attorney with a particular subject matter. Writing assignments can be on separate word documents or written as an email.

Regardless of the level of formality, you should treat each assignment as a golden opportunity to impress the assigning attorney with your research, writing and analytical skills. Here are a few writing tips most applicable to legal interns:

A. Confirm the requested format. Review your notes to confirm you deliver the work product in the form requested by the assigning attorney.

B. Outline. Before you toil over sentence structure and word choice, you must first organize the building blocks of your analysis. This requires an initial understanding on how the cases and the legal principles therein interact with one another. Here are just a few of the many questions that you may want to consider when creating your outline:

- Is there a seminal case or central statute?
- What are the legal doctrines at play?
- What are the elements of those doctrines?
- What are the jurisdictions of the cases that cite those doctrines?
- How do the various on-point cases interact with each other?
- Is a doctrine narrowed, expanded, or modified?
- Are any areas of this law undecided?
- Are there distinguishing facts?
- What is the procedural posture?

After answering these questions and applying the answers to the specific facts, you should be able to reach a conclusion and intelligently explain how you reached that conclusion. In other words, you should be able to answer the question asked and "show your math."

> *<u>Assignment Case Study (cont'd):</u> Your research yielded four cases and two provisions of the Bankruptcy Code that, in your opinion, are the most relevant primary authorities on the issue. You then draft an outline that synthesizes these resources to reach your conclusion.*
>
> *I. <u>Question Presented:</u> Should a Plaintiff's housing discrimination claim in the EDNY be dismissed pursuant to Fed. R. Civ. P. 12(b)(6) because that Plaintiff failed to disclose her claim in a prior bankruptcy for which she received a discharge?*

II. Conclusion: The Plaintiff's discrimination claim should be dismissed based on judicial estoppel.

III. Rule: With some exceptions, so long as the bankruptcy court relied upon the omission, judicial estoppel should be applied by the district court in deciding to dismiss the omitted claim.

A. Application of Judicial Estoppel

- *a. Carter (SDNY case) establishing elements of judicial estoppel.*
- *b. Carter elements adopted by EDNY in IBM case.*
- *c. Plaintiff met those elements (failed to disclose/received discharge)*
    - *i. Bally's case noting that receiving a bankruptcy discharge qualifies as reasonable reliance of the prior tribunal.*

B. Application of Judicial Estoppel to discrimination claim

- *a. Ibok supports the position that when an individual fails to disclose a claim in bankruptcy petition, judicial estoppel should bar their ability to bring that claim in district court.*
    1. *Ibok is SDNY case, but affirmed by Court of Appeals.*
    2. *Proposition in Ibok supported by Amash, which is NDNY case dealing with wage claim, not discrimination claim.*
    3. *There is no EDNY case on point.*

C. Potential exceptions to this rule

- *a. Ayazi seems to support the position that a pro se plaintiff whose estate was abandoned in bankruptcy should not be barred by judicial estoppel.*
    1. *Applied leniency to pro se litigants.*
    2. *Bankruptcy abandonment is formal process that must be considered.*
- *b. Plaintiff here was not pro se, weighs against application of Ayazi exception.*
- *c. We do not know if Plaintiff's estate was abandoned under Section 554 of the Code. Further inquiry needed before answering question completely.*

As you outline, you can begin to visualize which parts of the analysis have holes and what case law you need to fill those holes. Anticipate and answer questions that the assigning attorney may ask. Review your notes from the initial assignment intake and ensure that you covered everything. Continue the research and outline process until your outline is complete with no gaps in logic. Once you are comfortable with your outline, it is time to start writing.

C. Summarize comprehensively. You should draft each writing assignment envisioning that it will be read by a complete stranger ten years later. Or, more likely, the assigning attorney will read it at a time when they have forgotten many of the specific details. With that mindset, make sure that your question presented and applicable background facts are specific, defined, and understandable to any reader.

> *Assignment case study (cont'd): You start your memorandum email to the assigning attorney by summarizing the question presented:*
>
> *Hi Shelly:*
>
> *Earlier today, you asked me to conduct some research and write you an email answering the following question: Should a plaintiff's discrimination claim in federal court be dismissed on the pleadings if she had failed to disclose that claim in a prior bankruptcy petition?*
>
> *[You then review this summarization and expand on it to be more specific:]*
>
> *Should a housing discrimination claim filed in 2014 by an individual plaintiff in the United States District Court for the Eastern District of New York be dismissed on the pleadings because that plaintiff failed to disclose the discrimination claim in a 2011 bankruptcy proceeding for which she received a discharge?*

D. Follow CREAC. In practice, the attorneys typically want to know the answer up front so they can begin assessing their next steps. Without being robotic, your writing should loosely follow the CREAC (Conclusion, Rule, Explanation of Rule, Application of Rule, Conclusion) format so the attorney gets the information they need as quickly as possible. Starting with the conclusion will also highlight instantly whether you answered the right question.

E. Be comfortable proposing alternatives. Your writing does not need to be the last word on the issue. It should present whatever can be concluded at that juncture and highlight whether further exploration may need to be done.

> *Assignment Case Study (cont'd): Your research indicates that if a plaintiff's estate was "abandoned" by the bankruptcy court, this may prevent the district court from dismissing the discrimination claim. But the assigning attorney indicated that she did not know whether the plaintiff's estate was abandoned. This missing fact should be flagged in your email memorandum as follows:*
>
> *It is presently unknown whether the plaintiff's estate was abandoned by the bankruptcy trustee pursuant to Section 554 of the Bankruptcy Code or discharged for some other reason. Based on Ayazi, if the estate was abandoned, depending on the bankruptcy court's analysis, this fact may impact whether Rule 12(b)(6) should be applied by the district court.*

F. Perfect citations. This is critical for building and maintaining the trust of your assigning attorneys. With minimal review, they should be able to take your work and present it to a judge, superior, colleague, or client. Also, they will likely read your case law to confirm your analysis is correct. If your citations lead them nowhere, this will be frustrating, waste time, and erode trust.

G. Take your time. Interns tend to get overwhelmed by approaching deadlines, excited after finding the "perfect case," or eager to deliver positive news about research results. These feelings can prompt an intern to jump up from their chair and impulsively turn in a writing assignment before it is complete. Resist making this mistake. If you are finished with time to spare before the deadline, let it simmer for a while. Put the writing aside and think about it. Question whether you covered every angle and anticipated every question. You want the draft you turn in to be the only draft that your assigning attorney needs to read.

H. Be concise. A common downfall for intern writing is wordiness. Good legal writing is clear, unambiguous, and includes only the words necessary to establish the point. During an internship, you write for utility only. You will impress your assigning attorney with how quickly they can extract critical information from your writing. When you feel you're done writing, print it out, read it, and remove every superfluous sentence and word. Shorten phrases. Continue this process until your writing is as concise as possible without jeopardizing the message.

> <u>Assignment Case Study (cont'd):</u> *Your email memorandum is seemingly finished and you now read it through to try and shorten as much as possible. You review the following sentence:*
>
> *A plaintiff who has filed a bankruptcy petition has an obligation to set forth each and every asset that they have which may include, among other things, their real property assets, bank accounts and claims for unpaid wages that they have against their current employers or companies where they used to be employed.*
>
> *You then edit the sentence and change word choice to be more concise:*
>
> *~~A plaintiff who has filed a bankruptcy petition~~ Bankruptcy debtors ~~has an obligation~~ must ~~to set forth each and every asset that they have~~ list all of their assets ~~which may include, among other things, their~~ including real property ~~assets~~, bank accounts and wage claims ~~for unpaid wages that they have~~ against their current ~~employer or companies where they used to be employed~~ or former employers.*
>
> *Here's the new sentence:*
>
> *Bankruptcy debtors must list all of their assets, including real property, bank accounts and wage claims against current and former employers.*

I. Proofread aloud. The last step before submitting your writing assignment should be reading it aloud. This process requires you to read every word and listen to how it flows. It will reveal any "gremlins" that may have crawled into the writing, such as errant commas, missing articles such as "the" or "a," or misspelled words. These mistakes tend to creep into drafts that are cut and pasted, edited heavily, or written hastily.

J. Apply multiple coats of paint. It is unrealistic to expect that you are going to write your final draft on the first try. Rather, the writing process is analogous to painting a wall, with the first draft being the first coat of paint. Once you get it down on paper, paint over it again moving paragraphs and sentences to ensure it flows logically and transitions smoothly. Then paint over it again editing the word choice and sentence structure. As you're applying the last coat of paint, you should be catching grammatical errors. The more coats of paint/times you read and edit it, the more polished the final work product will be.

K. Ensure Your Work Product is Client/Court Ready. Sometimes interns can get used to or expect that their writing will be edited heavily by their supervising attorney. This should never factor into the amount of effort or finalizing you dedicate to your work. Regardless of whether your work will be modified, always submit work product with the mindset that it will be reviewed and analyzed by a judge, client, or another highly-critical end user. Don't rely on your supervising attorney to make it perfect. That's your job.

Oral Presentation of Your Legal Research

Attorneys are not praised for being good verbal communicators. They are *expected* to be good verbal communicators. So, you must be one also. Your internship is the perfect place to start sharpening that skill and develop a thoroughness of oral presentation. Inevitably each legal research assignment will involve a point where you need to communicate the results to your assigning attorney verbally. Don't just view these moments as practice, use them as an opportunity to impress your assigning attorney with your oral presentation skills.

Here are some tips for optimizing your performance while orally presenting your legal research assignment:

A. Outline the presentation. Write an outline of your "talking points" that you want to cover. Make sure it flows logically, highlights what is relevant, and gets to the point. Doing this will also slow you down and ensure that you don't start your presentation until you have thought it through and are ready.

B. Layer the presentation. Your talking points should cover all of the critical issues. But you should also prepare a second layer of material to add color and depth to your analysis. If your assigning attorney wants to probe deeper, be prepared to provide the titles and citations to relevant law, examples, illustrations, or any other information to help support your findings.

C. Practice beforehand. Depending on the amount of privacy you have at your workstation, you should practice reciting your presentation aloud. Doing this will cement the material in your mind, make your presentation more fluid and heighten your ability to think on your feet. Plus, hearing your own words will help identify statements that don't sound right and need to be tweaked.

D. Treat it like oral argument. Your oral presentation of legal research assignments may take place in various environments, such as in a conference room, hallway, office, sitting at your desk, walking, traveling on a train, or over lunch or coffee. Regardless, you should always treat these moments as if they are oral argument before a judge. This will ensure that you maintain a level of professionalism, formality, and efficiency in your presentation, and also will be great practice for when/if you are ever in front of a judge.

E. Use CREAC. Don't bury the lead. As with writing, your oral presentation should get the point and give the attorney the most important information first. After doing this, it should then be followed by your analysis.

F. Bring all authorities. Attorneys cannot simply take you on your word. As your supervisors, they are ethically obligated to check your work and confirm that it interprets and applies controlling law. Expect them to want to see all of the resources that you relied upon, including print outs of the case law, statutes, secondary sources and, if applicable, documentary evidence.

G. Be prepared for questions. In all likelihood, your oral presentation will be the beginning, not the end, of answering the research question. You want your assigning attorneys to challenge you on your understanding of the legal principles and facts. In these moments, you'll need to think on your feet and respond with the correct information in the right tone.

H. Don't lose your personality. Some interns make the mistake of trying to talk like their supervising attorney(s). There are some aspects of attorney's language that you should mimic, like their vocabulary, legalese and, of course, avoiding saying "like" or "um." But for the most part, you should stick to your own communication style. The more natural your delivery, the more persuasive you will be.

Reflecting on Your Performance

Remember to apply the science of experiential learning to each assignment for a deeper learning experience and to optimize your acquisition of practical legal skills. After you complete the legal research assignment, engage in reflective observation to solidify your understanding of the substantive material, as well as your performance and enjoyment of the assignment. Focus your "internal discourse" on describing what you did, analyzing your experience, deducing any conclusions and figuring out how you would do it differently in the future.

> *Case Study Assignment (cont'd):* *After you turn in your writing assignment and discuss the results with your supervising attorney, you engage in an internal discourse to reflect on the experience:*
>
> - ***What was I asked to do? What kind of problem was I asked to solve?*** *What practice area(s) were involved? How did my work fit into the bigger picture of that matter? What was I able to accomplish with my efforts? Did I enjoy the experience? Do I want to do this type of work for my career?*
> - ***What did I do well in conducting the legal research? What did I do poorly?*** *Did I research efficiently and exhaustively? Did I use all the resources available to me? Did I fully understand and assimilate the research before I started to write?*
> - ***What did I do well in my writing process? What did I do poorly?*** *Did my outline sufficiently lay the groundwork for my writing? Was my writing process efficient? Did I write clearly and concisely and answer the question asked? Did I miss any angles or were there holes in my analysis?*

- ***What did I do well in the oral presentation of my legal research? What did I do poorly?*** *Was I prepared and ready to present my results? Did I anticipate the right questions? Did I know the material well enough to think on my feet? Did I have all of the necessary materials with me?*
- ***What would I do differently for future legal research assignments?*** *Would I change my research strategy? Would I spend more time outlining? Would I ask more questions from the assigning attorney earlier in the assignment? Would I have proofread more thoroughly?*

Seek Feedback on Your Performance

After you submit — written or verbally — the results of your legal research assignment, be sure to follow up with your assigning attorney to get their feedback on your performance. This will communicate to the assigning attorney that you are dedicated to getting it right, relieve any anxiety about whether you did a good job, and enlighten you on areas for improvement. You can read further detail about how to seek, receive and interpret feedback in the next chapter.

Chapter 15

TWENTY TIPS FOR SUCCESSFUL PERFORMANCE

Achieving success during your internship is a game of inches. Of course, strong performance depends on your ability to be enthusiastic, demonstrate an acute attention to detail, upwardly manage your assigning attorneys and nail your research assignments. These are the building blocks of your internship performance.

But there is more you can do to ensure that you stand out from your peers, convince your assigning attorneys that you are a trustworthy professional and to extract the most value from the internship. In no particular order, here are twenty performance tips to help get the job done right.

1. Always Carry Notepad and Pen

Stop trusting your memory. In a busy work environment, it will be the first thing to let you down. Write down everything. Never leave your desk without bringing these two tools. If you are unexpectedly given an assignment and don't have a pad or pen, ask the assigning attorney for permission to take out your phone and email yourself the notes.

2. Get Names

When delivering documents, making a telephone call or dealing with a vendor, always get the name and title of the person with whom you are receiving information. This information may be asked of you from an assigning attorney.

3. Record Time Well

The client billing statement/invoice is perhaps the most important document generated by a law firm. They can work their hardest and achieve the best results, but without a detailed invoice setting forth what they did and how long it took, the firm won't get paid.

This means that law firm interns must develop good habits for recording their time. Whenever you finish a task, write down what you've done and how long it took. Do this as close in time to the performance of the task as possible to ensure that no time or details are lost. Use the following structure for your time entries:

First, pick an initial qualifier to explain the actual action that you carried out, such as: appeared; conferred with; prepared; researched; reviewed; drafted; conducted legal research; analyzed; telephone conference; discussed; interviewed; investigated; traveled; corresponded; compiled; or organized. Then, add a connector to describe the action and connect it with a particular matter, person or event, such as: for; from, on behalf of; in preparation for; regarding; to; with; as a follow up to; or in connection with.

This structure will ensure that your time entries have the same flow as attorneys in the office. Follow up with your assigning attorneys for feedback on your time entries to ensure that you are meeting their expectations.

> Side Note: Recording time is not just a private law firm concept. Many government organizations ask their attorneys to record their time so they can track resource allocation and make better policy decisions regarding staffing.

4. Maintain Confidentiality

Interns are bound by the same ethical standards of confidentiality as attorneys. Learn to abide by them. Set your smartphone to be password-protected. When sharing your internship experience outside of the workplace, be sure to not use specific names or other identifying information. When in doubt about whether information concerning your work assignments is confidential, err on the side of caution.

Not Good	Good
I reviewed thousands of pages of contracts between our client, Verizon Wireless, and its customers to determine whether they contractually promised not to increase surcharges.	*I reviewed thousands of pages of contracts between a large telecommunications company and its customers to determine whether they contractually promised not to increase surcharges.*
I had a telephone conversation with Bill Nichols regarding whether his secretary sent the documents.	*I had a telephone conversation with the company's CEO regarding whether his secretary sent the documents.*
I'm working on compiling information to help with a confidential SEC investigation into whether there may have been securities fraud committed in connection with Twitter's recent initial public offering.	*I'm helping the SEC investigate certain types of fraud in connection with IPOs.*

Also, keep in mind that organizations doing business across state lines or abroad may be subject to multiple layers of confidentiality laws. As an intern, you should be sensitive to which laws apply regarding your communications and transmitting of confidential information.

5. Write Memos to File

Whenever you perform a task on your own and there are certain pieces of information that you think may be helpful to a particular matter in the future, write it down, date it, explain where the information came from and place it in the file/save it on the computer network.

6. Be Responsive

Nowadays, especially in in private practice, attorneys check and respond to emails all hours of day, night, and weekend. Make sure to match the level of responsiveness that is typical among your co-workers and assigning attorneys. Also, confirming receipt of an assignment is important. A simple "I got it" or "OK" may put your assigning attorney at ease.

7. Think and Get Comfortable with Ambiguity

Good lawyers think about what they have read or heard before they take action. It may be difficult in a busy work environment, but make sure you carve out time to think, carefully and systematically, about your assignments.

Further, most assignments will contain ambiguity. You must embrace the fact that there won't always be a right answer. Attorneys learn to interpret and shape ambiguity in order to accomplish results for their client(s). Strive to do the same during your internship.

8. Make Mistakes Gracefully

You are going to make mistakes during your internship. This is a critical component of experiential learning. What is missed by most interns is that making a mistake presents an opportunity to set yourself apart — if you make your mistake *gracefully*. Doing so can show your introspectiveness, commitment to your work, and humility. It will demonstrate your potential and enthusiasm to improve, which creates a huge upside for hiring you. Here are four steps for making a mistake gracefully:

- **Step 1: Acknowledge your mistake.** Take full responsibility, even if it is questionable that it was all or partly your fault. Ultimately, your mistakes are the responsibility of your assigning attorney anyway. DON'T make excuses or get defensive.

> Side Note: Avoid saying "I'm sorry" if at all possible. If your intuition tells you that it is warranted, then apologize. Otherwise, apologies are emotional, backward-looking, and have no value in the workplace. Always be forwarded thinking.

- **Step 2: Identify the reason for mistake.** This is to demonstrate that you are self-aware and understand how to improve. If you can identify why you made the mistake, you can begin the process of ensuring that that same mistake is avoided in the future.
- **Step 3: Suggest a possible solution.** This will demonstrate that you are still engaged in the project, forward-thinking, and problem-solving oriented. You do not want to dwell on mistakes of the past. The most

important action you take is the next one.

- **Step 4: Never make the same mistake twice.** Repeat mistakes can give the impression that you are not focused or dedicated to improvement. This is the wrong message to send.

9. Work Hard

The practice of law is hard work that requires discipline, persistence, stamina, and sacrifice. These are common attributes of practicing attorneys and will, therefore, be expected of you during your internship. Here are a few tips to develop a reputation at your organization as a hard worker:

- **Work longer hours than your assigning attorneys.** If there are no employer restrictions on your working hours, be sure to get in earlier and leave later than your assigning attorneys.
- **Deadlines are the minimum.** If your workload permits and you don't rush, turn your assignment in earlier than expected and seek out further assignments.
- **Let your presence be known.** Physical presence in the office is important. If your workstation is located where your assigning attorneys can't tell if you're in the office early or late, be sure to make yourself visible by walking around, sending an email, putting on a pot of coffee, or turning on lights.
- **Work late when you can.** If you don't have plans and there are no employer restrictions on your working hours, work late. This will help build goodwill and a reputation as a hard worker. Having this reputation will lessen the negative impact if you have to decline working late in the future for plans that you cannot cancel.

10. Work Smart

While demonstrating that you are a hard worker is important, the raw number of hours spent in the office still will not be the best measure of your work performance during your internship. Your preparation, stress regulation, strategy, and execution will dictate whether your performance is good, very good or excellent. It matters how — not how much — you work.

11. Practice Good Email Etiquette

During your internship and for the rest of your career, you will communicate a great deal via email. During your internship, it is safe to assume that most recipients of your emails will be professionals with higher rank at the organization and more work experience. Keeping this in mind, consider the following:

- **Formal tone** — Err on the side of being formal. If an assigning attorney writes in a conversational, informal tone, then you may do the same. But unless and until you receive some indicator that informality is appropriate, write your email with deference and formality.

- **Mirror structure** — Mirror the recipient's email structure. If Sally writes "Dear Frank," at the beginning of her emails to you. Then your emails to her should open with "Dear Sally". If your assigning attorney writes quick one-liners with no greeting or closing, then you should feel free to do the same.
- **Call them what they call themselves** — If their full name is "Benjamin" but they sign their email with "Ben," feel free to call them Ben in the next email. If they do not sign their emails at all, and their signature block immediately follows the body of the email, then you should refer to them by their full, formal name unless and until they direct you to do otherwise.
- **Take care** — Write each email with the expectation that it will be sent to everyone in the world. Emails last forever. Think each one through carefully, proofread, ensure that it is concise, unambiguous, and does not contain grammatical errors.

12. Assess and Utilize Your Emotional Intelligence

Emotional intelligence is the ability to identify, assess and control the emotions of oneself, of others and of groups. Many human resource professionals believe that emotional intelligence (referred to as "EQ") is a more potent ingredient for success than intellectual intelligence. To boost your chance for success, be aware of the four areas of your EQ and assess where you may need to improve:

○ **What is your level of self-awareness?** Assess your own emotions and understanding of their origins. Doing so will decrease the possibility that you make rash decisions based on emotion instead of logic.

> *Example:* *Over the course of your internship, you failed to notice that you are becoming increasingly insecure about taking too long in performing assignments. Then, while performing a legal research assignment, you read a case that seems to be on point, print it out, jump out of your chair and run into your supervising attorney's office to present findings. The attorney then asks you if you Shepardized the case and you honestly respond "No." Not good. This is an example of being unaware of your own emotions and acting based on those emotions.*

○ **What is your level of self-management?** Think about how well you delay gratification and balance your needs with those of others. Doing so will help you avoid making impulsive decisions and elevate the needs of the organization over your own.

> *Example:* *Your office is moved from a very visible, highly-trafficked location in the office to an isolated cubicle on a different floor. There are no longer social interactions; it appears that nobody now notices you coming in early or working late and you are not included in meetings as often. Practicing self-management will help you overcome your frustration with being excluded and focus on your primary role — producing quality work product. To stay connected, you may have to be vulnerable and make extra efforts to visit people's offices, send emails and be outgoing around the office.*

○ **What is your level of social awareness?** Evaluate how attuned you are to other people's emotions and concerns, whether you notice and adapt to social cues, and if you can identify the power dynamics in your workplace. This will help establish connections and interpret the interactions between your co-workers.

> <u>Example:</u> *You are in a meeting with a staff attorney and the director discussing the staff attorney's results of an investigation. The director is rolling her eyes at virtually everything that the staff attorney says and speaking in a terse, agitated tone. You're not sure why. It's late in the day. The director then turns to you and gives you an assignment that you do not fully understand. You have questions. But your social awareness tells you that the director is not in a patient mood and wants the meeting to end. So you wait and ask your questions to the staff attorney after the meeting ends.*

○ **What is your level of relationship management?** This is linked to upward management. Assess how well and genuinely you get along with your co-workers, supervising attorneys, support staff and other interns. Your ability to manage conflict, inspire and influence people, and communicate clearly will help you develop relationships while you work.

> <u>Example:</u> *There is a paralegal at your internship organization that is impatient, blunt and can be an abrasive communicator. But he also has an enormous amount of wisdom about the "nuts and bolts" of litigation, such as how to use document review software, how to file documents, correspond with clerks, and organize and bind court filings. Having a high EQ will help communicate efficiently with the paralegal while under pressure, genuinely compliment his work product, be polite and consider his feelings. Your ability to build a relationship with him will dictate the level of support he provides to you.*

13. Be Generally Likeable

This is not a suggestion that you change who you are or be fake. It is simply an encouragement to be the very best version of yourself during your internship. You can be the brightest mind and the hardest worker, but if you are not liked, your experiences and relationships will be limited and your overall growth as a professional can be stunted. On the other hand, if you conduct yourself in an endearing manner, you will greatly increase your chances of achieving your internship goals. Here are some general tips on how to be likeable during your internship:

○ **Don't say anything negative about co-workers.** Refrain, at all costs, from sharing rumors, making statements about other people's actions, or telling stories about events in other people's lives.

○ **Listen and ask about others.** Encourage others to talk about themselves. Be genuinely interested in others and make them feel interested and important. Remember co-workers' names.

○ **Have a direct and assertive communication style.** Don't be aggressive. But don't be passive aggressive. Simply express yourself in a professional and direct way and remember to smile. Assert yourself gracefully when appropriate.

○ **Give others credit.** Humility is a virtue. Glory hogs are obvious and appear insecure. When you're in meetings or conversations, deflect credit to and praise your co-workers and assigning attorneys. This is an endearing, team-oriented trait.

14. Interact with Partners/Higher-Ups

While you may have the most interactions with support staff, and junior and mid-level attorneys, don't shy away from establishing relationships with the more senior members of the organization. Don't be discouraged if they appear too busy or work in a different area of the office. These individuals are influential in the organization and have lots of wisdom to share. Whether you simply pop into their office for an assignment or email them to ask for an informational interview, make sure you don't overlook the opportunity to develop relationships (hopefully working relationships) with these more experienced attorneys.

And **always** accept an invitation for coffee, breakfast, lunch, dinner or a drink from your assigning attorneys and/or their superiors. This applies regardless of whether you are actually hungry or thirsty. Personal interaction outside of the office is a great way to connect without distractions.

15. Be Prepared for Mini-Interviews

Consider your internship one, extended interview for an attorney position. Performing assignments for attorneys or even just walking the hallways may lead to quick, informal conversations about your background, qualifications and career aspirations. Always be prepared to answer these important questions as if you were in an interview for a position. And, as with formal interviews, keep in mind your audience when answering questions about your intentions for the future. If you are unsure about your career aspirations, consider that your internship organization may want to hear that goal is to eventually work for them.

16. Seek Feedback on your Work Performance

Feedback is the means through which your assigning attorney can help you get better. It may be direct or passive. It may be complimentary or harsh. It may come in person, through email or interpreted from the assigning attorney's actions. Either way, this critical component of your internship should be optimized in order to reduce anxiety about your work performance and help you improve. You must learn how to seek out and receive feedback during your internship.

Here are some tips on how to seek, receive and interpret feedback from your assigning attorney:

A. Better feedback comes soon after the assignment. The more time that passes after the assignment, the less the attorney will remember about your performance. To get the most specific, thoughtful reflections on your work performance, seek feedback from your assigning attorney as soon as practicable after you complete the assignment.

B. More likely to get feedback on on-going assignments. Some assignments are anomalistic, "one-offs" that you will never do again. Others can be ongoing or typical assignments throughout an internship. With the latter, an attorney is more likely to give valuable feedback because they will benefit from you improving the work product for future similar assignments.

C. Request a feedback session. Treat your feedback session like an important event and schedule a meeting. Email or approach your assigning attorney in person and ask them directly if they would meet for fifteen minutes to discuss your performance on a particular assignment. If they agree, ask them what date(s) and time(s) work for them and send them a calendar invite to confirm. There are three benefits to seeking feedback through a formal session: (1) it shows that you truly care about their feedback; (2) it may prompt them to prepare some detailed thoughts on your performance ahead of time thereby increasing the value of the feedback; and (3) setting a definitive meeting makes it more likely that the feedback session will actually happen. If they cancel, reschedule another date.

> *Case Study Assignment (cont'd): One day after turning in your assignment, you write an email to your assigning attorney:*
>
> *Hi Shelly:*
>
> *I was wondering if you had a moment to meet with me this week to discuss the legal research assignment that I submitted to you yesterday. I have some specific questions to ask and also generally wanted to get your perspective on how I performed.*
>
> *If you're open to this, please let me know what day(s) and time(s) work for you and I'll make myself available.*
>
> *Thanks so much,*
>
> *Chris*

D. Request feedback through specific questions. If your assigning attorney is too busy or unwilling to commit to an entire feedback session, then use this method to obtain feedback from them. Popping into their office, passing by in the hallways or a quick email can be an effective way of engaging your assigning attorney about your performance. As an illustration, consider the following exchange:

> *Case Study Assignment (cont'd): Your assigning attorney responds to your email:*
>
> *Hi Chris — I'm happy to discuss with you but I'm super busy this week. What is it you want to know?*
>
> *Shelly*
>
> *You respond immediately:*
>
> *Hi Shelly —*
>
> *Thanks for the quick response. The specific questions I wanted to ask were:*
>
> - *Did you find my writing concise and clear?*
> - *Did I answer the question asked?*

- *Was there anything that I missed?*
- *Were you able to use the work product? If not, why not?*

And, again, I generally just wanted to know your impression of my work performance.

My goal is to continue improving and having your insights on my work performance would help me accomplish that goal.

Thanks,

Chris

Your assigning attorney may have some insightful feedback for you. At the least, it may just lead to a simple confirmation that you did it correctly, which may be a huge relief. Their response requires little effort because you've simply asked a "yes" or "no" question. And, if the timing is right, it will open the door to a more complete discussion of your work product and maybe more assignments.

E. Prepare for the feedback. To the extent possible, prepare for your feedback session. Write down questions to ask about your performance, such as: (a) how well you answered the question asked; (b) whether you interpreted the law correctly; (c) whether your citations were in the correct format; (d) specific challenges you faced and how they would have handled them; or (e) whether your writing was clear and easy to read. Bring all necessary materials to jog their memory and reference during the feedback session.

F. How to receive direct feedback. If you are fortunate to have an attorney willing to spend their time providing you with one-on-one direct feedback on your performance, here is what you should do:

(1) Focus — listen intently to what they are telling you. Make eye contact as much as appropriate, exude appreciation and thirst for their thoughts. Write down questions that you may have while they are talking.

(2) Be thick-skinned — the assigning attorney wants to be able to give feedback efficiently and unemotionally. If they are concerned with hurting your feelings, you risk that they will withhold criticisms in future feedback sessions or, worse, not provide feedback at all. Again, DON'T make excuses or get defensive.

(3) Ask questions/get clarifications — don't just "uh hum" your supervisor while they are providing you with feedback. Make sure you know exactly what they mean.

(4) Thank the attorney for their time — it takes energy and time for an attorney to share their thoughts on your performance. It is typically a selfless endeavor for them. Acknowledge this and let them know that you appreciate it.

G. Decode "indirect" feedback on your performance. Some assigning attorneys may be non-confrontational or extremely busy and, therefore, do not give direct feedback. However, in these situations, there may still be cryptic or passive feedback available and it is up to you to interpret the message. Read emails and listen carefully for subtle critiques of your work. Ask for "redlines" of your work product so you can see the changes they made. Search for the final product and compare it with yours to see what was changed.

Also, after working at the organization for a few weeks or months, ask your assigning attorney to have a review session so you can obtain feedback on your work performance generally. This way, you can obtain feedback at a macro-level with an opportunity to correct mistakes and improve for the remainder of your internship.

17. Have a Customer Service Mindset

All practicing attorneys serve clients and customers. A lawyer's clients or customers may include individuals, businesses, government agencies, judges, in-house counsel, or other lawyers, such as partners, within a practice group. To be successful, lawyers develop a customer-service mindset. The most successful ones have clients who are satisfied from the representation. As an intern, you should adopt this mindset as well.

18. Take Responsibility for Your Work

Overall, your objective in upwardly managing your assigning attorneys should be to encourage them to view you as a colleague that they can trust to help them get the work done. To do this, approach your work as they approach theirs.

Attorneys are handed problems by their clients and expected to solve them. If you run into obstacles during an assignment, don't simply return to your assigning attorney, tell them of the obstacle and dump the responsibility back onto them.

> *<u>Example:</u> Your assigning attorney hands you a complaint and tells you to do some research. The client has been sued for breaching a commercial lease by failing to pay rent. The attorney explains that it's true the client hasn't paid, but it is because the landlord failed to perform certain renovation work. He then tells you to find cases where a landlord's failure to perform renovations excused a tenant's rent obligations. You spend two hours and cannot find one case that stands for that proposition. You go back to the attorney and report that there are no cases.* ***Wrong.***
>
> *Instead, continue researching analogous cases, try different states, counties, federal law, treatises, and read online articles. Take notes of what you did and what you learned. Then, if you still cannot construct any possible argument after all of that, report back to the assigning attorney all that you did, what you found, and possible suggestions on what the next steps may be, such as reporting back to the client that we have no defenses and should make a settlement offer.*

Pretend that there is no assigning attorney and you are solely responsible for delivering results to the client. Place that burden on yourself and become invested in the outcome. If, after exhausting all possible avenues you still cannot accomplish your objective, only then return to the assigning attorney and explain everything you did and why you came up short. And don't stop there. Suggest possible options about how to continue trying to solve the problem.

19. Have Fun

Your internship is a time to "test run" what it is like to practice law. And you should hope that you will enjoy practicing law. Consistently remind yourself that work should be fun and seek out moments to insert levity and laughter into your work day.

20. Be Yourself, Everyone Else is Taken

Don't allow your work environment to drown out who you are. While it is normal for an internship to be a transformative experience that shapes your professional persona and communication style, always stay true to yourself and be genuine.

Chapter 16

WINDING DOWN PROFESSIONALLY

In the days leading up to the end of your internship, it is important that you close out all matters in a professional way, plan for your future and leave a positive impression resonating with your assigning attorneys. Here are a few pointers for getting this done.

Close out Your Matters

First and foremost, your matters must not be negatively impacted due to your departure. If you are involved in projects/cases/deals that will continue on after you leave the organization, put time aside to ensure a smooth transition for the next person who assumes the file. This is a four-step process:

1. Organize the file. Compile all loose notes and place them in the physical file. Save all electronic documents and emails into the organization's online filing system. Tidy the files and folders. Make sure that whoever picks up the file can find everything they need. The highly-organized file should reflect the organized manner in which you managed the file.

2. Return documents. If you possess any documents that are a part of another attorney's file, bring those documents to them. Don't throw anything away unless you are absolutely sure there is already a copy in the file and the attorney does not want/need it.

3. Draft a closing memorandum. Put together an internal memorandum that includes the following topics:

a. The name of the matter;

b. The name and contact information of everyone involved with the matter (adversary, supervising attorneys, paralegals, secretaries, judges, clients, etc.);

c. The factual history, including relevant dates;

d. The procedural history (if a litigation matter);

e. Upcoming events with dates, times and other important information;

f. References to other important documents in the file; and

g. Any relevant strategy considerations.

4. Meet and discuss. Set up a meeting with the supervising attorney(s) handling each matter to discuss topics covered in your closing memorandum and answer any questions they may have.

The positive reputation you spent the entire internship building can be shattered if the next person picks up the file and it's a mess, things are missing, and the status of the file is a complete mystery. On the other hand, your legacy as an organized, thorough and trustworthy professional will live on after you're gone if you lay the groundwork for your replacement to smoothly take over.

Organization-Wide Announcement

Ask for permission from your supervising attorney to send out an organization-wide email announcing your departure and thanking everyone for the experience. Assuming it is not against some organizational policy (highly unlikely), this is a great way to give notice to everyone that you're leaving, provide your contact information to stay reachable in the future, and share some of your future plans. Here's an illustration of what a goodbye email may look like:

Dear Everyone:

As you may know, Friday is my last day here at Tarper Krinkley & Grogin LLP. During my time here, I learned much more than I could have imagined, grew immensely as a professional and developed some wonderful relationships. I truly appreciate all of the support that you have given me throughout my internship.

Now I will be returning to Northeastern University to finish my third year of law school and plan to take the New York and New Jersey bars after graduation. If anyone wants to reach me, my personal email is kgilmore@northeast.edu and my cell phone number is 234-555-5555. I hope to stay in touch.

Thank you again for everything. I will miss seeing you all every day.

All the best,

Kate

There's no formula for the perfect goodbye email. Just whatever feels right to you. Make sure you send this email at least one day before you leave or the morning of your last day. This will give people enough time to stop by your workstation and say goodbye in person without feeling rushed.

Meet to Say Goodbye to Specific Attorneys

You may never feel as close to these attorneys as you do in these final moments of your internship. Once you walk out that door, you will move on with your career and they will move on with theirs. You want to make the right last impression and plan for how to keep the relationship alive in the future.

Reach out to each attorney with whom you have a relationship to set up a definite time to talk and say goodbye. Prepare ahead of time for this meeting so you can efficiently and gracefully cover the following objectives:

- **Thank them for their participation in your internship experience.**

Tip — Think back on all that they did for you and be specific about what you appreciate. Did they offer you interesting assignments? Did they spend time with you going over your work product? Did they invite you into certain meetings for your benefit only? Your feedback on how they positively impacted your internship will give them insights into what you valued most and help them improve as supervising attorneys. Everyone wants to get better, including your assigning attorneys. It is also not uncommon to give a small gift or write a card to some attorneys as a token of your appreciation.

- **Reflect on your experience with them.**

  Tip — Think about the work experiences that you shared with the attorney. Be specific about your perspective on the experience and what you learned/how you were impacted. If something was difficult or frustrating, try to articulate how you will apply the lessons learned from that experience in the future.

- **Solicit their final feedback on your performance.**

  Tip — Again, be specific. Try to stay away from generally asking "How did I do?" Lead them to the feedback by asking more tailored questions like "Did I demonstrate that I understood the concepts?" "Did you feel like you could trust my work product? If not, why not?" "What could I have done better in that situation?" Emphasize to them that their constructive criticism is most valuable because you are dedicated to improving. Remind them that you have thick skin.

- **Ask for their advice on the next steps in your career.**

  Tip — Tell them how you plan to spend the rest of your time in law school. Where you plan to work next. What classes you are going to take. The states in which you plan to take the bar. Tell them your rationale behind each decision and ask them if they agree or have any insights. If you haven't already, ask them to reflect on the decisions that they made during law school.

- **Request specific assistance from them.**

  Tip — They know that you will need help in accomplishing your goals. This is no mystery. If you feel close enough to them, make a specific request for the help that you need. Ask them if they approve of you listing them as a reference for future employment. If you are interested in a particular practice area, industry or location, ask them if they know anyone who might be a valuable contact and ask for an introduction.

- **Plant seeds for the future.**

  Tip — Keep in mind that no matter how close you may feel with your supervising attorneys, your commonality has been that you were employed by the same organization and worked together. When your internship ends, this commonality will be gone and you'll need to replace it with something new. Think of ways that you could stay in touch with them. Is there a conference approaching that might be of interest to both of you? Are you going to be in town in a few months and want to grab lunch? Is there an article that you want to write to which they might want to contribute? Think of them as their colleague moving forward. How are your interests and values aligned? Where might you be able to connect in the future? Be the one who proposes how to keep your professional relationship alive.

Nobody likes saying goodbye. These conversations can sometimes be awkward, and even the most social and charismatic attorneys can buckle or get nervous. Make sure you plan ahead of time and take the lead if appropriate. Have specific topics to cover, prepare (and even rehearse) things you want to say and approach these final meetings with professionalism. This will cement the right professional image of you in their mind.

Let Your Future Intentions Be Known

If your internship experience confirmed that you would like to work at the organization in the future (for another internship or as an attorney), don't hide this fact. Identify the decision-maker(s) and approach them in-person. Be direct and assertive and let your intensions be known:

"Hi Alan, I had a great experience here and I wanted to let you know that if there was ever an opportunity to come back and work here again, I would like to be considered. So please keep me in mind."

There is nothing wrong with saying what you want. If there is a position available, you are essentially asking for it. If there is not currently one available, you are removing all doubt that you do not want it. You never get what you don't ask for. Make sure the organization knows what you want.

Clear Your Plate for the Last Day

Your last day should be dedicated only to engaging in relaxed personal interactions with your co-workers. You do not want to be stressed out or rushing to get work done on your last day. Plan ahead so all of your work is finished by the time your last day rolls around.

Update Your Resumé

While your internship experience is fresh in your head, sit down and update your resumé. Write down every project on which you worked, each specific task that you performed and, all of the successful results that you achieved. Write with as much detail as possible. You can always shave it down when you are tailoring your resumé for the next position.

Re-Evaluate Your Career Considerations

Reflect back on your internship experience. Think about what you liked, didn't like, and what you learned about yourself. Go through your career considerations and evaluate whether anything has changed about your perception of yourself and career aspirations.

- *What are your values? Have they changed at all?*
- *What do you want to achieve as a legal practitioner?*
- *Who do you want to serve as a legal practitioner?*
- *What types of matters do you want to work on?*
- *What are your interests? Is there anything new that you would like to explore?*
- *What practice areas are most interesting to you?*
- *What type of organization(s) do you want to work at next?*
- *Did your internship experience meet your expectations? If so, how? If not, why not?*
- *Has your desired lifestyle changed in any way?*
- *What was the lifestyle of the attorneys at your internship organization? Would you want their lifestyle?*
- *Did you learn that you had any new strengths? Weaknesses? Preferences?*
- *What did you learn about your personality?*
- *Was there any consistent feedback from attorneys that provided new insights about your abilities?*
- *Are your career aspirations the same as they were before the internship? If so, how did the internship confirm them?*
- *Are your career aspirations different? Why have they changed?*

These are big questions to which you may not have all the answers. But now that this internship is over, it is time to start thinking about these career considerations again, looking ahead to new challenges, refining your goals and making the right decisions to continue forging your path towards a successful career.